ALONG THE
PENISTONE LINE

PETER THOMAS

First published in the United Kingdom in 2007 by
Sutton Publishing, an imprint of NPI Media Group Limited
Cirencester Road · Chalford · Stroud · Gloucestershire · GL6 8PE

British Library Cataloguing in Publication Data
A catalogue record for this book is available from the British Library.

ISBN 978-0-7509-4619-3

Typeset in Ehrhardt 11/12pt.
Typesetting and origination by
NPI Media Group Limited.
Printed and bound in England.

Contents

Foreword

If you are looking for a book on Yorkshire there is always a good selection on the dales, the moors, the Pennines and the coast, but far less attention has been given to the small area of countryside around the Penistone Line. Not only is this area small, but – dare it be said – unfashionable as well, it needed a sympathetic editor and plenty of optimism to be considered for publication. Sutton Publishing had both, hence Along the Penistone Line.

Looking back on this adventurous project, and an adventure it really was, this journey had everything: landscape, rivers, buildings, excitement, unexpected happenings and, of course, the Penistone Line. Life will not be the same for the author and the book invites its readers to share the experiences described here.

By following in the author's footsteps, you could learn to drive a steam train, go underground to a coal seam, cruise and walk canals, see some of the best porcelain ever made in this country, watch the 'Big Melt' at the Magna Science Adventure Park and, of course, ride the Penistone Line.

The map below shows the Penistone Line, its station stops and the surrounding road network. Following the introductory sections, including the courageous building of the line, the area's features are described and illustrated, beginning at Huddersfield. Each station on the line and its local attractions follow, ending at Sheffield. Happy exploring!

Peter Thomas, 2007

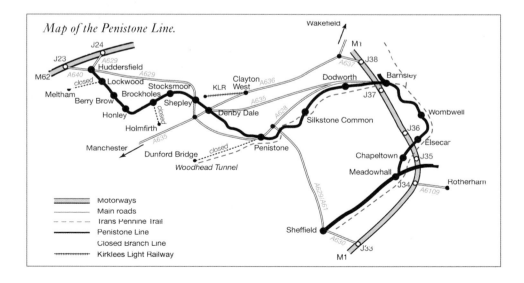

Map of the Penistone Line.

▬▬▬	Motorways
────	Main roads
‒ ‒ ‒	Trans Pennine Trail
▬▬▬	Penistone Line
▬▬▬	Closed Branch Line
▪▪▪▪▪	Kirklees Light Railway

Building the Penistone Line

Yorkshire's industrial development would never have been possible without using its river system to transport raw materials and manufactured products. It soon became clear that the building of canals would be necessary to extend and improve the waterways; three were cut across the Pennines, the Rochdale, the Huddersfield Narrow Canal, and the Leeds–Liverpool Canal, the most important of all. Begun in 1770, it took over thirty years to complete. Without it coal could not have been transported in the large amounts that were needed and the Yorkshire textile industry would not have expanded as it did.

Of course, transport by canal was a great improvement over carriage by packhorses, but it was a slow system and railways began to compete with canals by the 1840s. The 'canal mania' period was over and 'railway mania' was about to begin.

The first public railway was George Stephenson's line from Stockton to Darlington, and it showed how important rail transport would be for both passengers and freight. Investors rushed to put money into railway construction; both lines and stations multiplied. Sheffield had two stations (Bradford and Wakefield still have) and routes were duplicated as well.

The Manchester and Leeds Railway was completed in 1841; its route had no difficult gradients, but it did not extend to Halifax, Huddersfield or Dewsbury, reaching Leeds via Normanton and Wakefield. Competition became fierce, with many companies seeking authority to build lines, and mergers followed; the majority of schemes were unwise to say the least and ideas to build, then link short branch lines would seem illogical today.

The rail network was so unplanned and became so complicated that companies were forced to seek running powers to use lengths of each others' tracks and stations to complete their journeys. This was the situation as companies competed for business within south and west Yorkshire and for services to Manchester.

What was originally known as the Huddersfield and Sheffield Junction Railway, later to be amalgamated with the Manchester and Leeds Railway (then renamed the Lancashire and Yorkshire Railway Co.), was granted authority to build a direct line from Huddersfield to Sheffield. A 'deal' that granted running powers by the Lancashire & Yorkshire Co. and the London & North Western Co. to each other over lengths of their respective lines was followed by a joint station being built at Huddersfield – and what a beauty it was!

Work began on the Huddersfield to Penistone section in August 1845, at least on *some* of it, as negotiations to purchase land went on interminably at the same time as building took place.

Mytholmbridge viaduct. (B.C. Lane)

The plan at Huddersfield was for the Penistone Line trains to join the Manchester route inside the tunnel there, then to enter the station. Parliament refused permission for this on grounds of danger; as an alternative the great Springwood cutting had to be constructed and a junction provided outside the tunnel.

This was typical of the way costs escalated as problems were encountered: there were 2¼ miles of tunnels, four major viaducts and fifty-seven bridges. The purpose of the line was to provide a direct route to the south and to shorten the journey from Huddersfield to Sheffield. To the company, almost any costs appear to have been acceptable.

Structures were on a massive scale, too. The Lockwood viaduct, just south of Huddersfield, crossed the River Holme; its 34 arches made it one of the largest in the country, its parapet being 136ft above the river. It required enormous quantities of stone, but fortunately these were available as a result of the cuttings made close by, along the line.

As well as the cuttings, steep embankments had to be constructed in addition to the viaducts and tunnels. It was in one of these, the 1,631-yard long Thurstonland Tunnel between Brockholes and Stocksmoor, that a train on the line's opening day came to a halt. Half the train was all that the locomotive could take on to Stocksmoor, with the remaining coaches having to wait in the tunnel for rescue. The rails were wet and the under-powered engine could not cope with the load and the incline.

Frustrating as that was at such an embarrassing public moment, there was fortunately no danger to life and limb as there was at Denby Dale, where the viaduct had unwisely been built of timber; it collapsed in 1847 in a gale. The lesson was not learned. A timber replacement also collapsed, to be rebuilt finally in stone in 1882.

There was an even more spectacular collapse at Penistone in 1916, when an engine that had just arrived with a train from Huddersfield was on the stone viaduct while running round the train to be coupled up for the return journey. The driver and fireman noticed that the tracks were beginning to give way, jumped off and escaped injury.

As the viaduct arches failed, the engine fell into the deep valley below, ending up on its side – a photographer's dream! Within months the viaduct had been rebuilt and the track re-laid; a tribute to the hardy workmen who often had to contend with bad weather. It was thought at the time that the Penistone collapse was the result of heavy rain that had affected the foundations of the viaduct. It has to be remembered that the Penistone Line had to cross four river valleys; Colne, Holme, Dearne and Don, so it is not surprising that problems arose not only in the course of construction, but also in operating the line.

Three branches were built along the route from Huddersfield to Penistone, the more rural part of the line:

1850: Brockholes to Holmfirth,
    2 miles, closed in 1965
1869: Lockwood to Meltham,
    5 miles, closed in 1965
1870: Clayton West Junction near
    Shepley to Clayton West,
    3½ miles, closed in 1983

Holmfirth
The 2-mile branch line from Brockholes to Holmfirth, with an intermediate station at Thongsbridge, close to New Mills, was more easily and quickly completed than expected. Trains could have run from Huddersfield to Holmfirth by the end of 1849 had there not been a delay in the completion of the Paddock viaduct south of Huddersfield. The line eventually opened in July 1850.

Huddersfield: Paddock viaduct. (B. Barnsley)

7

Turntable on the Holmfirth branch line. (B.C. Lane)

There were several proposals to extend the Holmfirth branch to Holmbridge in the early days, but nothing came of them. A double track had been laid and there were warehouse and goods yard facilities; textiles, metal castings and parcels traffic, combined with a well-supported passenger service, suggested a bright future for the line. Towards the end of the nineteenth century, improvements were carried out; a turntable had been built in 1883 and, it is thought, a water tank had been installed. Any thought of the extension to Holmbridge had obviously been abandoned by then.

Thongsbridge was a busy station too. Its goods yard handled heavy coal traffic as well as products from Thongsbridge and Albion Mills nearby. Runaway accidents seem to have been few – and those were mainly at Brockholes (originally named Holmfirth Junction), when Holmfirth passenger coaches were being 'slipped' to make connections with trains to or from other destinations. One very curious runaway incident took place at Holmfirth when a coach ran into the turntable pit, ending up badly damaged and unfit for further use on the line.

After the Second World War, with the growth of road transport, British Rail published plans for the closure of the branch; by the 1950s there were only four trains a day each way on the Holmfirth line.

Crash at Penistone, 1916.
(By kind permission of Barnsley
Metropolitan Borough Council
Archives and Local Studies
Department)

Meltham

The branch lines were short, but they still had their disasters just as the main Penistone Line did. Building on the Meltham branch began in 1864, and shortly after geological problems showed themselves. The route passed through areas of shale made unstable by water from hill springs; landslides were to be expected and the first took place within a year – in August 1865 – inside Netherton Tunnel. Others followed at Dungeon Wood, north of Butternab Tunnel.

Little more than half a mile from Netherton station was another station: Healey House, whose name came from the large country house nearby. To ensure that the view from the house was not ruined, the line was concealed below a covered carriageway.

Meltham branch runaway.

A halt was built for employees at Meltham Mills, just outside the town, but general public use of the Meltham branch fell into decline as road transport developed.

Clayton West
The original 3½ miles of the Clayton West branch line were planned to be extended like the Holmfirth branch; Darton might well have been the destination, giving access to the Barnsley district with its coal traffic. The extension never took place and was perhaps doomed from the outset, as there was a delay of about six years in starting work on the line; construction was slow and it was seven years before it was completed.

The Clayton West Junction was built three-quarters of a mile south-east of Shepley and Shelley station on the main Penistone line and there was one stop, Skelmanthorpe, en route to the terminus at Clayton West. In order to handle coal traffic there were sets of sidings at Clayton West Junction, Skelmanthorpe, and at Clayton West itself. At Skelmanthorpe there was a goods yard, sidings that dealt with Emley Moor colliery traffic and private tramways linking the station with small local collieries.

Because of its adjacent colliery, Clayton West's shunting yard was a busy one; a tramway provided a link with Park Mill colliery. Both stations had single platforms for passengers.

There was only one tunnel on the route, Shelley Woodhouse, 511 yards long; the main feature of the Clayton West branch was the gradient which fell 1 in 70 most of the way to the terminus. This was not a problem when empty coal wagons were being moved eastwards, but loaded trains being hauled uphill from Clayton West or Skelmanthorpe towards the main Penistone line were a different matter. Rules had to be made to cover the possibility of an engine being unable to take its load to the top of the incline and being forced to halt. The closure of the branch came in 1983.

It may be that the builders' success in overcoming the many problems in completing the Penistone Line minimised in the company's mind possible future dangers to trains using it. Some of the accidents towards the end of the nineteenth century were the result of weaknesses of the rolling stock, causing derailments. Others might not have happened but for the severe gradients that increased the possibility of 'runaways'.

In June 1858, stationary loaded coal wagons at Honley broke free and began running away towards the viaduct at Lockwood. Soon travelling at high speed, they smashed into a Leeds–Manchester passenger train, killing three people and injuring a number of others.

Only a few years later, in 1866, a tragedy was narrowly averted when some passenger coaches at Lockwood ran free and accelerated dangerously away, just coming to a halt on reaching the Huddersfield viaduct.

Clayton West arrival, 1954. (H.C. Casserley)

The twentieth century had its moments, too: on 23 June 1958, empty passenger carriages that had been stored in a siding on the Meltham branch line above Lockwood began running down the incline towards the main line. Passenger services on the branch had long since been withdrawn, so one can imagine the astonishment of the signalman to see the runaway. Fortunately he acted promptly and 'according to the book' by alerting a colleague at the next signal box.

To avoid the possibility of a collision the runaway was diverted on to a goods loop and from that to a short length of line that ended with buffers. These were swept aside as the carriages ploughed on, ending up embedded into the booking hall on the other side of the road. Miraculously no one was hurt; apart from being covered by debris, even the booking office staff were none the worse off.

Railways in exposed countryside are always vulnerable in bad weather; the Penistone Line seems to have attracted more than its fair share of adverse conditions and the delays that result. This perhaps explains why those who know about these things are fond of asking if Penistone station is the coldest in England.

Over the years there have been a number of examples of trains stuck in snow. One episode reached the headlines because it involved the only 'prestige' train on the line. It was the South Yorkshireman, the daily through express from Bradford to London (Marylebone), which became stuck in a snowdrift near Denby Dale viaduct in February 1958. Another famous train in those days of steam followed the same route from Sheffield: the Master Cutler was the fastest train to the capital in its day.

11

History of the Penistone Line

When Dr Beeching's report on the re-shaping of the country's railways was published in 1963, the days of the Penistone Line appeared to be numbered. Total closure of the route between Huddersfield and Penistone was recommended in the report, but fate took a hand.

Recently appointed Minister of Transport, Barbara Castle decided to refuse consent to the closure of the line from Huddersfield to Penistone and of the branch to Clayton West, the first of the Penistone Line reprieves. Her 1966 decision was based on the need to avoid adding to congestion on the roads; the number of commuters using the line from some of the rural stations was not large and made the Minister's decision surprising, but of course, welcome.

In the years that followed, British Rail sought financial savings wherever they could, this included reducing the frequency of trains and closing stations. The gradual decline of the service made the line more vulnerable than ever, particularly after the closure of the freight service from Penistone to Manchester in 1970. This route via the Woodhead Tunnel was of importance in the early days of northern railways when coal from Yorkshire was in great demand to provide power for Lancashire mills. The loss of this and other freight services meant that passenger numbers became all-important if the line was to continue to operate.

In 1974, Passenger Transport Executives (PTEs) were established for South and West Yorkshire; their role has been to identify the travel needs of people in their areas and to promote on their behalf the best possible systems of public transport within the resources available. South Yorkshire was originally only interested in 'their' part of the route south of Penistone, while West Yorkshire limited its interest to the section from Huddersfield to Denby Dale and then only one track.

A 1980 proposal for the closure of the Penistone Line was eventually agreed by the Minister, who suggested that consideration first be given to diverting the existing Penistone to Sheffield section via Barnsley to take advantage of passenger traffic there. The closure was postponed until an experimental scheme had been agreed between British Rail and the South Yorkshire Passenger Transport Executive. The re-opening of Silkstone Common station on the diverted route was part of that scheme.

By now the Huddersfield, Penistone and Sheffield Rail Users Association was on the scene. The Association had been formed in March 1981 to fight closure proposals and to ensure that a collective voice would be heard on behalf of passengers; it does considerably more than this today.

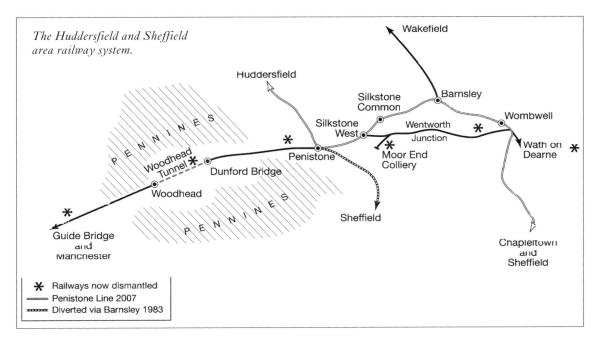

The Huddersfield and Sheffield area railway system.

The arrival of the Huddersfield, Penistone and Sheffield Rail Users Association (HPSRUA) was just in time to meet yet another closure threat, now from the West Yorkshire PTE, wishing to close the section from Huddersfield to Denby Dale. The PTE and British Rail had failed to agree respective funding for the northern section and the struggle began again.

Objections to closure were vigorously sought and lobbying was intense; a successful challenge by the Chairman of the Transport Users Consultative Committee was mounted to British Rail's claim that only passengers who travelled between Huddersfield and Denby Dale could object to the proposed closure, and this delayed action for a year.

A public meeting about the closure proposal was held at Huddersfield in October 1985. Convincing evidence was produced by the Rail Users Association (RUA) about the hardship that would arise from closure and presented positive proposals for the development of the line. The result was that both South and West Yorkshire PTEs had agreed by 1987 to support their respective sections of the line and closure was averted yet again.

By that time Silkstone Common station had already been re-opened and a new station was completed at Berry Brow in 1989. Once revival and renewal were underway, all sorts of efforts were undertaken to attract passengers; stations were improved, track was replaced and an hourly timetable was introduced.

After all its troubles, the Penistone Line deserved some luck; it came with the popularity and growth of the huge Meadowhall shopping complex. Opened in 1990, the Interchange station handles large numbers of shoppers and workers going to and from the shopping centre and provides a link with the local bus and Supertram service.

The role of the HPSRUA in 1981 in meeting threats of closure to the Penistone Line is no less important today through monitoring the performance of the railway to protect the users.

Features and illustrations in 'Track Record', the HPSRUA's newsletter issued three times a year, informs users of activities on their behalf: fares, services, station and track maintenance, safety, new trains – even ticket machines. For an example of an annual subscription giving good value for money, look no further.

The Penistone Line: A Community Railway

The railway closures following the Beeching report in 1963 had a serious effect on many country areas. Although most rural lines had few passengers and little freight, the railways were a lifeline for rural communities; buses were almost non-existent, having to negotiate narrow winding roads and use round about routes to make as many calls as possible to pay their way.

By the 1990s the future of rural railways had become a critical issue; a study was carried out and made a particular recommendation that was to influence the future of the Penistone Line. This was to form community rail partnerships embracing train operators, local authorities and communities themselves. Local people could participate in a whole host of ways that publicised the railways and by organising activities that brought passengers into the area.

Arising from this at a meeting in September 1993 was the Penistone Line Partnership, a voluntary organisation which works with the Yorkshire Passenger Transport Executives, Metro and Arriva Trains Northern to promote and develop the Penistone railway line. Its aim is to develop projects and activities which benefit local communities along the line and increase awareness of the train service.

These have included regular guided walks from stations along the line, aimed at those who like a friendly, easy-paced walk. Several villages such as Denby Dale and Emley have their own self-guided village trails.

The Music Train has proved a great hit: the 20.18 departure from Huddersfield on six Mondays in June, July and August has live music. Blues, rock, folk, trad jazz – even Tango Tzigane have been played. The atmosphere is complete with a bar on board; the 21.14 return train from Sheffield arrives at Huddersfield at 22.54.

The Penistone Line Partnership (PLP) has published an attractive illustrated leaflet 'The Penistone Line Pub Trail', featuring pubs along the line that are within a short walking distance of Penistone Line stations.

Northern Rail has recently published a new and updated version of the 'Penistone Line Guide', a leaflet giving an account of the rail journey from Huddersfield to Sheffield and illustrating the changes that have been made since the first edition of the guide in 1993.

In the Spring 2006 issue of the 'Penistone Line Express' there were reports of passenger numbers on Penistone Line trains: an average of 74 on the extra

Penistone Line Music Train. (B. Barnsley)

(Northern Star) trains prior to Christmas without passengers having transferred from other services. About 200 people travelled to see Father Christmas.

In January 2006, Burns Night was celebrated with Northern Regional Director Malcolm Brown clad in kilt and piping the haggis on board the train at Huddersfield; the Good Egg Band entertained passengers en route. On leaving Penistone, haggis, neeps and tatties were served and, courtesy of Northern Rail, a wee nip was offered.

Northern Rail have re-launched their station adoption programme for 2006; at level 1 passengers are committed to monitoring stations and reporting defects, while at level 2 groups are invited to take on responsibilities such as gritting platforms and gardening.

A transport development scheme operating as part of the PLP is the Community Car Club, 'Our Car, Your Car', which for a membership fee offers a car pool service at an hourly rate and mileage charge. Members book a car via the internet or telephone, go to the car and drive away. This is a 'not for profit' rural car club that operated so successfully at Slaithwaite and Marsden from central locations that it has been extended to Holmfirth; there is even a choice of vehicles.

It hardly needs to be said that the PLP is an 'ideas' organisation which began without any funding at all. Its pioneering work with schools and youth clubs, its arts and history projects show what is possible. Offers of help from Women's Institutes and individuals have made a great difference to passenger service quality and there has been plenty of goodwill, with Northern drivers becoming members.

15

Denby Dale arrival from Huddersfield, 2006. (B. Barnsley)

The PLP Chairman, Neil Bentley, is a driver with Northern Rail. In issue no. 41 of the 'Penistone Line Express' he described what he saw from his driver's cab: new long welded rails with concrete sleepers to provide a smoother ride, improvements to foot crossings at Silkstone Fall Woods, clearance of line-side vegetation and renewal of signalling equipment in the Attercliffe and Brightside areas.

Another article in the same issue describes improvements to three of the major stations on the Penistone Line: Sheffield, Barnsley and Huddersfield. There is also news of the free town centre bus service from Huddersfield railway station.

So PLP members are well informed on serious matters affecting travel on the line, while at the same time updated on fun events like the Santa Train, Easter Eggspress, poetry workshops, even a musical revue 'Brief Encounters on the Penistone Line'. Look for children's artwork too, notably at Huddersfield station.

For the serious shopper, the extra Sunday 'Northern Star' trains have proved so successful that they are becoming a permanent feature. The community railway is very much alive!

Communities that have lost their branch lines

Once very much part of the Penistone Line through their branches, some communities were left high and dry due to the closures that took place in 1965 and 1983. Increasing car ownership and better public bus services encouraged more travel and made Huddersfield seem much closer; changes in local government, vesting control in Kirklees Metropolitan Borough Council based in Huddersfield, also seemed to affect local attitudes.

If these changes originally appeared likely to diminish the identities of villages and small towns previously fiercely independent, this did not happen; the main reason was local peoples' realisation of the need to protect and preserve their own heritage. Schools became involved, as well as civic and historical societies. Town trails were planned, printed and signposted, places of interest marked and public footpaths charted.

People started visiting these communities: there may not have been a university, millennium gallery or massive football stadium to see, but sites of importance and interest that help to understand a distant past, explain the present and point to the future, are to be found.

Holmfirth

The only remaining visible sign of Holmfirth's former railway is the tall-chimneyed station building that once included the stationmaster's house; it is now a private residence. The single platform, trucks, goods shed and warehouse have all gone, replaced by a Jehovah's Witnesses' Kingdom Hall church and a new housing development.

With some difficulty, stretches of the track bed further out of town can be walked. It involves going up Station Road towards New Mill and negotiating a steep, stony and overgrown path that leads down towards the River Holme; the original incoming line followed the course of the river and went through Berry Bank woods to Holmfirth station.

In the outward direction trains ran to Brockholes (about 1½ miles away), the junction on the main Penistone Line. There was just one intermediate station at Thongsbridge; the journey to Brockholes took seven minutes, and from here to Huddersfield a further 23 minutes.

Although the branch line was well patronised both by passengers and freight (particularly coal), the decline of the textile industry and the development of road transport were bound to bring change. Excursion trains were always very popular, but the cancellation of regular Sunday services showed the way things were going. If diesel units had been introduced the line might have been saved but the last passenger steam train ran in 1959, much lamented.

The former Station House at Holmfirth.

From early times the people of Holmfirth and surrounding district engaged in farming and forestry; spinning and weaving took place in cottages and a reputation for fine worsted production grew. The many streams, supplemented later by reservoirs, provided power for waterwheels as factories took over the domestic cloth industry in the Holme valley. Tragically, the bursting of reservoirs after heavy rainfall brought damage to Holmfirth on several occasions; in 1852 a massive flood swept through the town, killing 81 people. The use of steam power and the coming of the railway transformed Homfirth's economy, but the town's long-term future was to be changed in the most unexpected ways.

Many people who visit the Tourist Information Centre near the traffic lights on the Huddersfield/Woodhead road are surprised at the large display of humorous postcards there. They will not know until they visit Holmfirth that this is where the picture postcard, especially the 'cheeky' version, became a big industry, all because of one man: James Bamforth. He foresaw photography as a money-making venture and went into film-making (silent, of course) in the late nineteenth century; as an artist he began to design postcards which families newly able to travel by train could send to friends and relations from their holidays.

The old Bamforth factory is no longer in production, the business having been bought by a Leeds company, but the name and reputation survive. Also surviving is the Holmfirth Picturedrome, facing the river in the town centre and once

The Holmfirth Picturedrome.

owned by the Bamforth's, where silent films were shown; it has been restored and now offers a range of musical and film events.

The other name forever associated with Holmfirth is the popular television programme *Last of the Summer Wine*, which brings thousands of tourists to the town each year and is big business, too. Shops have opened to take advantage of the tourist trade and a bus takes visitors to see all the scenes familiar to regular viewers. A running commentary on board the bus points out the sites: 'Sid's Café' is just below the church where the formidable Ivy serves tea; by a bridge over the river is Scarfold, Nora Batty's house. Her front door is at the top of a short flight of stone steps, with Compo's place below and next door. There is even a 'Wrinkled Stocking' tea room.

Filming for *Last of the Summer Wine* takes advantage of many locations round Holmfirth. Of special interest is Jackson Bridge, the first location used, where Foggy, Clegg and Compo were regularly

Sid's Café, Holmfirth.

thrown out of the White Horse because of their behaviour. High up on a ridge behind the pub is a row of former weavers' cottages; immediately you see them you will recognise the television home of Clegg and, next door, that of Howard and his eagle-eyed wife, Pearl.

As a small town, Holmfirth bursts at the seams with visitors in summer. It pays to park as quickly as possible: just off the A6024 Huddersfield road, via School Street, is a large car park (and a supermarket). School Street is about 200 yards from the Victoria Street traffic lights which are a regular pain. Look for the 'P' sign coming in to town from Huddersfield, and turn left.

Make the Tourist Information Centre one of your first stops: their leaflet 'Holmfirth in Pennine Yorkshire' and their list of eating places are a great help and so are the staff!

> *For Holmfirth take the A616 from Huddersfield to Honley, then fork right at the traffic lights. Follow the A6024 to Holmfirth*

> Or *Penistone Line to Huddersfield*
> *Take bus services 309–316 from the bus station*
> *Services run every 10 minutes. Journey time depends on route*
> *Buses call at Honley, Penistone Line station*

Meltham Mills.

Meltham

When Meltham was recorded in the Domesday Book (as Meltha) it was, no doubt, a small settlement. Like others it grew, especially as industry developed; in the case of Meltham the river provided power for the textile firms that established themselves here.

The Penistone Line branch might never have been built had it not been for the importance of Meltham Mills to the whole district. The 1860 proposal to build the line (three possible routes considered) was designed to serve the town and Meltham Mills. Some might say that Meltham Mills *was* Meltham.

While there were several textile firms in the town at that time, and small mills carrying out processes such as fulling and dyeing, other industries such as coal mining and brick making were important but were not on a large scale. The first train ran in 1869.

The branch line itself was on a small scale; starting near Huddersfield, just north of the Lockwood viaduct, it passed near Beaumont Park and ended at Meltham, 3½ miles from the junction at Lockwood. With stops at Netherton and Healey House, the journey took 17 minutes. Before reaching Meltham station, trains stopped at Meltham Mills Halt for the convenience of workers, some of whom came from as far away as Huddersfield; it was an un-staffed halt and tickets were issued from an office at the Mills.

The Meltham Mills Halt closed in 1934 when United Thread Mills took over the Jonas Brook company and moved some work elsewhere. In their turn, United Thread Mills were taken over by J. & P. Coates and again work was transferred out of the district. Today, nothing remains of Meltham station; most of the site is

Old railtrack, Meltham.

occupied by a supermarket and its car park, although a neglected area on the corner of Station Street and Mean Lane appears to have been part of the goods yard.

Beyond the supermarket is a development of modern houses covering the goods sidings; roads on the estate give access to a public footpath running along the former railway track, which now makes a pleasant country walk.

It is sad to think of the loss of so much employment at Meltham following the decline of textile production at Meltham Mills, then by the closure of the David Brown tractor plant there. In earlier days the Brook family provided work at the Mills and gave the community facilities including a school, church and vicarage.

Meltham has one of those familiar crossroads layouts which make an exploration of the town a simple matter. The major roads radiate from the market place at the crossroads: from Huddersfield a right turn leads down Station Street to the former station site (now the supermarket) while turning left on Holmfirth Road leads past the primary school with its sculpture tree. Almost opposite are terraces of workers' houses: Calmlands were built by the Brook family, Wetlands by the Co-op.

Tree sculpture, Meltham.

21

Further down the hill at the crossroads is a guide stoop (ancient milestone); here, Millbank Road on the left passes the lower part of Meltham Park before joining Meltham Mills Road. Here it is possible to see the huge size of Meltham Mills, now partly occupied by a variety of industrial units.

Passing Meltham Mills' church and school, a left turn leads uphill on Huddersfield Road past the entrance to the Robert Ashton Memorial Park. Meltham Hall, former home of the Brook family, is now an apartment building for elderly people, standing behind high hedges.

Further uphill, Meltham's main civic buildings are conspicuous where the shops begin. First is the Carlile and Mechanics Institute, now the Civic Hall, which incorporates a branch library (ask for a copy of the 'Meltham Historical Town Trail'); next door is the Town Hall with a tall clock tower. The Town Hall opened in 1898 and was donated by Edward Brook of the Meltham Mills family, who gave so much to the town. The Institute was donated by J.W. Carlile who was a partner at Meltham Mills; behind the Institute is a free public car park.

The crossroads are only a few steps away; if open country and walking appeal to you Meltham is surrounded by high moors. The Pennine Way can be reached via two routes, to Marsden and to Standedge.

For Meltham take the A616 from Huddersfield to Lockwood then continue on the B6108

Or   *Penistone Line to Huddersfield station, then bus service 324*
Service runs every 15 minutes. Journey time: 20 minutes

Or   *Penistone Line to Honley station, then bus service 911*
Hourly service. Journey time: 40–45 minutes (scenic route)

Clayton West

Clayton West was a tiny community in the eighteenth century, typical of the agricultural scene in the Dearne Valley with spinning and weaving being carried on in cottages; there was waterpower, of course, on the River Dearne and waterwheels would have driven machinery in the mills that populated the area.

By 1847 the population had reached about 1,000 and the area benefited from increasing prosperity, influenced by better communications, especially the Wakefield turnpike. The packhorse bridge near the Woodman Inn at Clayton West is a reminder of days gone by. Mills dependent on coal for power had the advantage of supplies at Park Mill, near today's Clayton West station on the Kirklees Light Railway.

As always, industrial development relied on ambition and investment; in Clayton West this came in the form of John Kaye, a textile manufacturer. In the nineteenth century, rail transport came with the opening of the Clayton West branch of the Penistone Line.

Its closure came in 1983 when there was virtually no coal left to carry; the line's existence depended on it in spite of a well-used passenger service.

Clayton West is no longer the industrial village it once was, with a colliery and numerous textile mills; most people commute out of the village to work. Wakefield is easily reached by car or bus.

Near to the Kirklees Light Railway station is a luxury leisure home company specialising in designing and building timber homes – popular with customers having leisure time and the money to go with it.

Unlike the other Penistone Line branches, Clayton West enjoyed a new life after its closure – as a 15in gauge steam railway; a great tourist attraction.

For Clayton West take junction 38 off the M1 then follow the A637 towards Huddersfield. Pass the Yorkshire Sculpture Park and West Bretton
At the next roundabout take the A636 towards Denby Dale

Or   Penistone Line to Denby Dale
Then rural bus service 935. Hourly service. Journey time: 5 minutes

Huddersfield

During the eighteenth century the focal point of Huddersfield's growing wealth was the dockland called Aspley Basin, the terminus of the Ramsden, or Huddersfield Broad Canal, which connected the town and its industry to the Calder & Hebble Navigation at Cooper Bridge in 1780. When the Narrow Canal was completed through the Standedge Tunnel into Lancashire and the two canals met at Huddersfield in 1811, the Aspley Basin with its wharves and warehouses became even more important.

Here, cargoes had to be transhipped to and from the large keels that travelled the Broad Canal into narrow boats. Coal was unloaded into canal-side mills through 'taking-in' doors and warehousing became a vital activity.

Aspley Basin, Huddersfield.

24

Former warehouse on the Broad Canal.

Today the area has been transformed: the Basin has a marina with pleasure craft that navigate the canals. Many of the canal-side buildings remain but, now converted, are part of Huddersfield University. One historic warehouse still stands, probably the oldest building in Huddersfield town centre, built by Sir John Ramsden in 1788 for storing wool: it has been converted into luxury apartments. There are taking-in doors on four levels and the remains of a winch hoist can be seen just below the gable.

Parking is available on the north side of Wakefield Road, so for comfort and convenience it is wise to go down the steps and follow the towpath under the busy road to pass the warehouse on the opposite side. Next to it is a crane with a base of cast iron and a heavy stone as a counterbalance. Another crane is a little further along next to university buildings and the former slipway where a canal loop once provided more wharf space.

Student bridges cross the Broad Canal occasionally, so there is plenty of activity up above; the towpath has quiet and level walking past former mill buildings that line the canal and which have been converted for university use. Reminders of the past are everywhere: metal mooring rings are set at regular intervals along the wharves where boats were tied up.

Huddersfield: Aspley Basin

Ramps paved with 'setts' remain where cargoes, especially coal, would have been wheeled or carried through taking-in doors from the boats.

At Lock No. 1, where the Broad Canal ends, a notice welcomes visitors to the Narrow Canal – and it certainly does become narrow here – although the towpath continues and there is a footbridge over the lock. Everything has been restored and painted: a welcome sight. Next to the lock is a by-wash carrying surplus water and acting as an overflow channel if the water in the upper lock should threaten to reach a dangerous level.

The canal and towpath (which also served as a wharf) pass under the stone Commercial Street bridge with more huge mills only touching distance away; conversion work is still continuing along here.

Queen Street South bridge is the last on the trail. Metal steps lead up to street level, where there are direction signs for rejoining the towpath. It is not easy to find this spot from the town, as Queen Street South hardly exists on street maps, so there is a strong case for using the towpath and making the bridge a 'turn round' point for canal walkers. Before doing so, look up at the arch of the bridge: there you will see the Ramsden coat of arms, weathered it is true, but a sign that the family, and Sir John Ramsden in particular, should be remembered for the construction of the artery that brought wealth to the town.

Lock on the junction of the Broad and Narrow Canals.

Canal bridge with the Ramsden coat of arms.

Do not leave the Aspley Basin area without taking a short walk north along the towpath from Wakefield Road; an alternative would be to walk along St Andrew's Street to Quay Street. The tall six-storeyed Turnbridge Mill and a nearby mill chimney mark the position of a unique bridge over the Broad Canal. Once this was a swing bridge from which the mill was named, but was replaced in 1865 by a vertical lift bridge designed to use a combination of wheels, chains and counterweights to lift the deck of the bridge and allow canal traffic through below. Notices warn that it is a 'Weak Bridge', but road vehicles can pass over it with care.

> *For Aspley Basin take the A629/642 Wakefield road*
> *Follow the nearside lane after the ring road roundabout*
> *At the first set of traffic lights turn left into St Andrews Road*
> *The car park is about 200 yards on the left*
>
> *Or   Penistone Line to Huddersfield*
> *Bus service 235 or 239 from the bus station*
> *Services run every 15 minutes. Journey time: 5 minutes*
>
> *Or   Walk from Kingsgate shopping centre*

Huddersfield: Castle Hill near Almondbury

Standing guard over the northernmost miles of the Penistone Line and only 2 miles from the centre of Huddersfield is the vast bulk of Castle Hill. Standing at over 900ft high, the summit, like Ingleborough, was once crowned by an Iron Age hill fort, although Castle Hill was occupied centuries earlier than that. Prehistoric communities had to defend themselves and crowded together behind the strongest fortifications that they could build, often just banks and ditches.

Hill forts like this appear to have been enlarged and developed as time passed, communities became larger and there was more contact with the world beyond the hill. At Almondbury's Castle Hill the bank and ditch were strengthened. The site was occupied for about 4,000 years until around 400 BC, when a fire caused the fort to be abandoned, probably due to the damage caused to the fortifications. It was left unoccupied during Roman times and remained so until the De Lacy (or de Laci) landowning family built a stone tower (or keep) on the highest point in the 1400s.

The De Lacy medieval castle was strengthened and enlarged to enclose a bailey which would have been defended by its own bank and ditch as well as by the neighbouring keep. A lower bailey was also added on the south side still further from the keep; evidence suggests that an attempt was made to found a small town, but it did not last. The area may have been used as a cattle enclosure too.

In the event of an attack by force, the defenders would have been dependent on water supplies, not easy at a height of 900ft. The discovery of a medieval well is not surprising, although as far as is known there was never a siege of the castle.

Castle Hill and Victoria Tower.

Berry Brow station carving. (R.M. Casserley)

The only military use for the castle in more recent times seems to have been as a beacon site to warn of danger, such as the Spanish Armada in 1588 and in the course of the Napoleonic Wars. Today's tower, which brings the total height on Castle Hill to nearly 1,000ft, is not a real castle at all.

Like the Emley Moor television mast, the tower can be seen from far away; as the Penistone Line trains leave Huddersfield it remains close by on the left.

A good view is from Berry Brow station, the second stop on the line; from there it is but a short, pleasant walk to the tower, a strongly recommended route. Berry Brow once had unusual station signs cut into the stone face of the cutting in which the platforms stand. Two local sculptors, Thomas Stocks and his son John Charles carved them out in 1836. John's showed a train passing under an arch that was supported by two pillars. The carving went to the York Railway Museum in 1963, but is now on display at the Tolson Museum in Huddersfield.

> *For Castle Hill follow the A642 (Wakefield) road from Huddersfield*
> *At the A629 junction fork right on to the A629*
> *Opposite the Star Inn, Fenay Bridge,*
> *follow brown signs for Castle Hill through Almondbury*
>
> *Or   Penistone Line to Berry Brow*
> *Leave station towards Castle Hill*
> *Join Lady House Lane*
> *There are various alternative routes to the tower*

Huddersfield: Cooper Bridge and the Huddersfield Broad Canal

Huddersfield's success in becoming a prosperous textile town owes much to Sir John Ramsden; in particular his 3¾-mile Broad Canal, completed in 1780 – even now carrying his name – which linked the town with the national canal network.

At Cooper Bridge, the Broad Canal joins a river section of the Calder & Hebble Navigation. The A62 Huddersfield–Leeds road crosses the River Calder here, just yards from Canal Lock No. 1. Notices are posted to warn boaters of a dangerous weir on the river, protected by a floating boom. The Calder & Hebble Navigation continues from here to Sowerby Bridge and via the Rochdale Canal to Manchester.

Although the waterways merge at Cooper Bridge, it is by Lock No. 2 at Colne Bridge that the Broad Canal begins to impact on the local scene. It was always an important place because an ancient road (Dalton Bank Road) came from Almondbury and Dalton and continued northwards over the River Colne to Leeds.

At Colne Bridge close to the Royal & Ancient pub, formerly the Spinners' Arms, the B6118 road swings uphill towards Grange Moor and Barnsley; in the Bradley and Huddersfield direction there are three bridges within yards of each other crossing in turn the River Colne, the Huddersfield Broad Canal and the railway line from Huddersfield to Leeds.

Cooper Bridge, canal and weir.

Cooper Bridge, lock no. 1 and lock-keeper's cottage.

Steps and a narrow footpath both lead comfortably down to the Broad Canal towpath. Towards Huddersfield, industrial buildings crowd the route. Craft had to negotiate nine locks before reaching the basin: in spite of that, the canal was a huge benefit, avoiding the necessity of loading or unloading keels at Cooper Bridge and finishing the journey by road wagons. The construction of the Narrow Canal and its tunnel through the Pennines at Standedge near Marsden, and completed 30 years later, linked Huddersfield directly with Manchester and brought even greater advantages.

From Colne Bridge along the towpath to Locks 2 and 1 and Cooper Bridge, the scenery could not be more different. If you are looking for a gentle country walk, this is one to enjoy: an easy firm towpath surface, two locks, a bridge carrying the Huddersfield to Leeds Railway and a riverside that would look great in a feature film. At Cooper Bridge there are many good photographic points around the lock; a big bonus is the lock-keeper's cottage, beyond which is access to the bridge carrying the Huddersfield–Leeds road. The cottage is a good illustration of a building whose fitness for purpose satisfies every important rule of design; it appears likely to have had a warehousing function as well as that of a home for the lock-keeper.

The weir close to Lock No. 1 makes the river un-navigable from this point, so craft heading towards Wakefield have to continue under the road bridge, then via a lock to enter the river further downstream.

31

There is no doubt that Colne Bridge was once a much larger community than it is now; there were terraced houses on both sides of Dalton Bank Road and a Methodist Chapel. A forge is known to have been worked by the bridge and many people living at Colne Bridge will have worked at the cotton mill that stood near Lock No. 2. It was here that seventeen young girls aged between 9 and 18 were killed in a disastrous fire in 1818; they are remembered in the churchyard at Kirkheaton (see p. 46).

After the local mills closed, people moved away from Colne Bridge and the settlement declined; most of the houses have gone, the Methodist Chapel too. By 2006, houses remained only on the pub side of Dalton Bank Road; on the other a lonely byway leads off in the direction of the River Colne, probably once having served the backs of the demolished terraces.

For Cooper Bridge and Colne Bridge follow the A62 from Huddersfield to the crossroads at Colne Bridge. Turn right into Bridge Road. Parking is difficult unless you patronise the Royal & Ancient public house

Or   Penistone Line to Huddersfield. Then bus service 219 from the bus station. Alight at Bridge Road
Hourly service. Journey time: 20 minutes

Huddersfield: Greenhead Park

Ten years before the land at Lockwood that was to become Beaumont Park had been donated by H.F. Beaumont in 1879, a campaign had already begun to acquire land near the centre of Huddersfield for use as a public space. In May 1869 Thomas Denham, a draper and alderman, opened the campaign at a Town Council meeting. He was aware that land owned by Sir John William Ramsden at Greenhead was being considered for sale as an area for housing and in Denham's opinion it was ideal for development as a public park.

Such was the urgency of the matter that he took a three-year lease on that part of the Ramsden estate with the public being allowed free access to the land; the council took over the lease in 1873 and eventually bought 30 acres for a public park in 1880 at a price of £30,000 – Sir John Ramsden making a personal donation of £5,000. By then, activities including an annual firework display and concerts by famous military bands had become established.

In 1927 further land was bought, bringing the total area to about 33 acres; on this extension tennis courts, bowling and putting greens were laid out. Near the main entrance conservatories were built. These were restored in 2006.

When you walk round the park, look out for the trunks of one or two of the elm trees that still stand despite suffering from Dutch elm disease; most have been cut down altogether. These remaining trunks, stripped of their bark, have had domestic scenes carved on their pale inner surface by Colin Wilburn, an artist-in-residence at Sunderland's Riverside Project who has carried out similar work elsewhere in Yorkshire. The easiest one to find in Greenhead Park is by the main pathway close to the war memorial which shows a furled up umbrella and a pair of shoes. Colin calls it 'Up against'.

The war memorial at Greenhead Park, Huddersfield.

Over the years a number of proposals for development in Greenhead Park were discussed by the council but were abandoned on grounds of cost, and some features such as the boating lake have been eliminated. The bandstand remains however, as does the paddling pool and many of the attractive flowerbeds. A miniature railway has been added, facing the café and the tennis courts.

At the upper end of the park is the war memorial surmounted by a huge cross; this is on a mound approached by a series of steps and encircled by a stone balustrade. At the opposite end and facing the conservatory is the statue and memorial to the Huddersfield men who fell in the South African War of 1899–1902.

Huddersfield believes Greenhead Park to be one of the finest Victorian parks in England. Lack of adequate funding to keep it in proper condition led to a successful Lottery Grant application for a comprehensive restoration – a £4m plan was approved and work is scheduled to begin in 2007. This will include a

33

South African war memorial.

Tree carving by Colin Wilburn.

newly-designed bandstand, restoration work on the war memorial and the Italian Garden fountain. There will also be a new ornamental lake, along with new park gates and railings.

> *For Greenhead Park take the A640 Rochdale road out of town*
> *Cross the ring road and follow Trinity Street*
> *Pass signs for Greenhead College (no traffic entry)*
> *Take the next left into Park Drive (this is a one-way system)*
> *Kerbside parking, more space can be found at the top end of the park*

> *Or* *Penistone Line to Huddersfield*
> *Turn right and cross George Square*
> *Continue to the traffic lights*
> *Turn right and cross the ring road*
> *Follow Trinity Street to the park's main gate*

34

Huddersfield: Longley Old Hall

Longley Old Hall, a Grade II listed manor house situated 1½ miles from the centre of Huddersfield, passed by marriage to the Ramsden family who retained ownership until 1976. The house however has its origins in the fourteenth century, when it was owned by the Wood family. Robert Wood was first mentioned in connection with a deed in 1330.

The family's wealth grew and John Wood was the largest landowner in Almondbury in 1532. In 1543 we know that William Ramsden had married Joanne Wood and was renting Longley Old Hall from Joanne's brother: the date when he bought Longley is not clear.

In the late Tudor period the medieval hall was almost entirely rebuilt, not for the last time, as in the nineteenth century it was partially demolished and rebuilt, afterwards resembling John Ramsden's Tudor Hall.

Seen from the south (the Castle Hill direction), Longley Old Hall appears today to be a four-gabled house with mullioned windows. It is a misleading impression because so many changes have taken place; in particular, under the stone cladding is much of the original timber-framed building.

Some of the oldest remaining parts of Longley date back to the mid-fourteenth century and it is clear that the early medieval house followed the customary plan

Longley Old Hall.

Beamed bathroom at Longley Old Hall.

of a central hall, flanked by cross wings; the so-called H-plan. One wing would have been a servants' wing and probably weaving would have been carried on there; on the opposite side of the house was the family's private wing. During one of the re-building phases the central area of the house and the wings were brought into line, resulting in the smooth line of the front of today's house.

An important feature of a large medieval house was its Great Hall, open to the roof, which was supported by a complex network of timbers. As building techniques developed, upper floors began to be inserted in these halls and this was done at Longley at some stage, creating additional space known as a 'solar' – a private family area.

At Longley the roof timbers include huge beams which support king posts that go up to the ridge of the roof and take its weight. No doubt it was once thatched. Oddly, it is in the main bathroom where an outstanding piece of the roof timbering can be seen. As time passed and alterations to the house were made, parts of the timber framing were covered up and only come to light during investigations or restoration.

Of special interest and importance are the Dining Room, with fine oak beams and Tudor oak panelling, and the Drawing Room, also beamed and where there were two painted panels. In wealthy households painted religious scenes with captions were often placed in important rooms as evidence of the family's faith.

As research work continues at Longley Old Hall, more information is being uncovered about its history. Just as important, the past is being re-created too, with an Elizabethan knot garden, which has been established at the front of the house.

Visits to Longley Old Hall can be arranged. Further details can be obtained by calling 01484 430852.

For Longley Old Hall take A629/642 from Huddersfield to Shorehead roundabout
Take the outside lane marked Almondbury, into Somerset Road
Take the second right to Lowerhouses, passing the Mason's Arms
At the T-junction turn right into Lowerhouses Lane
Longley is on the right after 20 yards

Or   Penistone Line to Huddersfield. Bus service 327 from the bus station
Stop at junction of Lowerhouses Lane and Wood Lane
Service runs every 20 minutes. Journey time: 10 minutes

Huddersfield: Ravensknowle Park and Tolson Memorial Museum

Anyone travelling on the A642/A629 Wakefield/Sheffield road from Huddersfield will have seen, 1½ miles east of the town centre, a park shelter unlike any other. Handsome and historic: not only on account of its handmade bricks, ten tall pillars, clock tower and cupola, but equally because of its ancestry.

Like other textile towns, Huddersfield once had a Cloth Hall, built in 1766 by Sir John Ramsden, where cloth produced by local weavers was marketed. It was demolished in 1930 but, fortunately, some of the materials from it, including pillars from its central hall, its clock tower and cupola, were saved. The bell used to mark the beginning and end of each day's business was also salvaged. The rescued material was incorporated in the park shelter.

A more appropriate location for it could not have been found: Ravensknowle Park, which houses the Tolson Memorial Museum. The land, known as the Ravensknowle estate, was bought by a banker, Thomas Wilson, whose intention was to build a house on it; instead he sold it to his nephew, John Beaumont, a textile manufacturer. In 1860 John Beaumont built a mansion, Ravensknowle Hall, on the land in the Italianate style; it was believed to have cost £20,000, a massive sum in those days. The Hall's imposing façade and its fine ashlar stonework show that the money was well spent.

Museum shelter.

On Beaumont's death it passed to his daughter, who eventually sold it to her cousin, Legh Tolson. When he retired in 1919 and moved to the Lake District, Tolson offered the estate to Huddersfield Corporation as a memorial to his two nephews, both of whom were killed in the First World War. His wish was that the house should become a museum and the grounds a public park; the official opening took place in 1922.

Over the years alterations and extensions to the museum building have taken place, but mercifully the main rooms have remained as John Beaumont had them built and decorated. One look at the reception area, entrance hall and staircase reveals the high standard of workmanship and the high quality of materials that went into this building.

Tolson Museum.

The original policy of the museum was that it should concentrate on local aspects, illustrating the main factors at work in the environment. This has been maintained and important collections have been acquired in the fields of natural history, archaeology and 'bygones'. There is an extensive textile display showing how production methods have changed and in the rear of the museum is a large transport collection. In fact, the museum well-illustrates the history of life in the Huddersfield area from prehistoric times to the present day.

An extract from the Kirklees Museum leaflet reads: 'Discover how the wealth from factories gave Huddersfield the chance to become "The Town that bought itself".' It does not add 'from the Ramsdens', but that is what it means. The Ramsden family gained through inheritance, marriage and financial power, a significant 'empire' in Huddersfield and the surrounding area.

It all began in the sixteenth century, when William Ramsden bought the manor of Huddersfield; his son bought the manor of Almondbury and although the family chose to fight on the wrong side in the Civil War, they were wiser in their support of William of Orange in 1689. John Ramsden was made a baronet as a result; he had already obtained a market charter from the Crown in 1671, an essential step in developing trade. The Ramsden coat of arms is on the Huddersfield Market Cross and the family name appears as a street name, also through the name of their main seat at Byram, near Pontefract.

Having established the Cloth Hall in 1766, they also built the Ramsden (or Broad) Canal, that connected Huddersfield to the Calder & Hebble Navigation at Cooper Bridge. Together with the Narrow Canal that opened up markets to the Colne valley and through the Standedge Tunnel to Lancashire, Huddersfield was able to take a major part in the business that came as a result of the Industrial Revolution. Buildings all over Huddersfield arose through the activities of the Ramsden family.

By the end of the nineteenth century there was disquiet on the Town Council that increasingly prosperous Huddersfield, now conscious of its importance, had a powerful landlord; only with his permission could many decisions affecting the town and its people be taken.

When the Borough celebrated its Centenary Pageant in 1968 one display said it all: '1920: Huddersfield bought itself for £1,333,000'. That was the sum finally agreed with the Ramsden estate in 1920; following an Act of Parliament giving the necessary powers, Huddersfield had bought itself.

The story of the way that wealth from factories made this possible is one that any museum would want to tell and the Tolson Museum does so admirably.

> *For Ravensknowle Park take the A642/629 for 1½ miles*
> *Look for the lodge on the right and the park shelter*

> Or *Penistone Line to Huddersfield*
> *Bus services 233–240 to Waterloo*
> *Regular services. Journey time: under 10 minutes*

Huddersfield station and George Square

Described by Sir John Betjeman as 'the most splendid station façade in England', the building was designed by J.P. Pritchett of York and completed in the Greek style in 1850.

The huge central block framed by six Corinthian columns has steps leading to today's entrance hall. Colonnades on either side of the portico lead to two pavilions planned as booking offices for the two railway companies that served Huddersfield: the Lancashire and Yorkshire Railway and the Huddersfield and Manchester Railway and Canal Co. Their crests are above the entrances of the pavilions, now pubs: the central block is today's main booking hall.

There is no doubt that the completion of the station and the plan to develop George Square in front of it were the factors that influenced much of the modern planning and building of 'new' Huddersfield.

Old buildings were demolished: one in particular, the George Inn, was re-erected elsewhere and allowed for the present George Hotel to be built. This was the first new building in the Square,

The George Hotel, and below, the station portico.

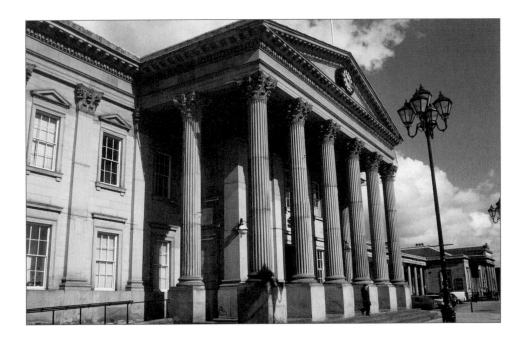

39

Rugby League plaque at the George Hotel.

designed by William Walden. John William Street was built to lead directly from the Square to the Market Place.

The hotel has a symmetrical façade; its corners are accentuated by its corner stones (quoins), the ground-floor stonework being rusticated or chamfered at the joints to give solidity. Standing as it does at the corner of the Square, its importance is obvious.

In the lounge is a plaque and display recording the foundation at the hotel of the Northern Rugby Football Union on 29 August 1895; this later became the Rugby League. On 30 August 2005 a Rugby Heritage Centre was opened at the hotel.

J.P. Pritchett, who designed the station building, was also responsible for the Lion Buildings close by on John William Street. Completed in 1853, the name comes from the massive lion on the roof above the central doorway of the Lion Arcade; although originally of stone, today's lion is a reproduction in fibreglass.

On the fourth side of the Square, facing the George Hotel, are the Britannia Buildings completed in 1859. It has a striking visual impact with the Royal Coat of Arms on the centre of the parapet, surmounted by a massive figure of Britannia. Symmetrical, its front has six boldly framed windows on either side of the arched entrance. Rustication of the lower stonework is again used by the local architect William Cocking with the added surface dressing called Vermiculation, a covering of indentations thought to resemble snail tracks.

The Lion Arcade.

Huddersfield: Almondbury and the parish church of All Hallows

What is now considered a residential village some 2 miles south-east of Huddersfield was once a considerable township, the focal point of a huge parish of about 50 square miles. Within the township were two villages: Almondbury and Newsome. The latter away to the north-west beyond Castle Hill (see p. 28) was, as its name suggests, founded after Almondbury.

The granting of a Royal licence in 1294 for a market at Almondbury to serve farmers and weavers makes clear how important the township was. It was 1671 before a similar charter was obtained for Huddersfield where advantage was being taken of its situation alongside rivers and developed quickly during the Industrial Revolution. Weavers' cottages in Almondbury are evidence of textile manufacture long before Huddersfield's mills were built.

Opposite All Hallows Church is Wormall's Hall on Westgate. Above the door are the initials I.W.M. (Isaac Wormall) and the date 1631, when the ground floor was covered in stone; the house is much older than that. The jettied first floor remains timbered; it has vertical studs linked by diagonals, together with mullioned windows, giving a silhouette that is quite

Wormall's Hall.

The 1631 doorway.

unforgettable. By 1631 timbering was falling out of favour for house building; oak was in short supply and stone's lasting quality was making it both fashionable and popular for new building and restoration.

All Hallows Church is large and shows how much Almondbury was expected to grow; in the end the village was overtaken by Huddersfield, but All Hallows' fourteenth- and fifteenth-century features suggest continuing prosperity.

The earliest written evidence of a church at Almondbury is an entry in a register in York dated 1231, but there is no doubt that an older church did exist, perhaps a tiny wooden one, or a stone one built when the de Lacys were Lords of the Manor here. A great rebuilding of the old church took place between 1486 and 1527, the cost being met by the Beaumonts of Whitley (see p. 45) and the Kayes of Woodsome, who were granted chantry chapels in the church.

Many of the fifteenth-century decorations and most of the stained glass were removed at the Reformation, but nineteenth-century restoration returned the church to its pre-Reformation beauty. The exterior of the church is in the Perpendicular style: battlements and pinnacles along the nave and on the tower the wide windows with mullions. This confirms the fifteenth-century rebuilding date.

It is the painted oak ceiling in the nave which brings many visitors to All Hallows. Where the panel bearers meet are carved bosses with designs relating to

All Hallow's Church, Almondbury.

the Passion of Christ, including a sponge and a spear of the Crucifixion, the letters IHS and a cross. Painting was done in 1936 to add to the beauty of the carvings. A Gothic-style carved inscription runs round the ceiling in the form of a passion poem: an appeal from Christ on the Cross. It carries the date 1522 and an attribution 'Geferay Dayston is the maker of this', which suggests that he was a carver. Like pictures in stained glass, the bosses relate the events of the Crucifixion to those who were unable to read.

The oldest parts of the church are the tall, narrow, so-called lancet windows of about 1220 on either side of the sanctuary. Before the nineteenth-century extensions they were external windows. There is a fine hammer-beam roof in the choir, but the interior furnishings and the organ are from the nineteenth and twentieth centuries.

The Lady Chapel at the end of the north aisle is alternatively known as the Kaye Chapel because the family monuments of the Kayes of Woodsome are there; their stained glass in the chapel's east window is some of the oldest glass in the church.

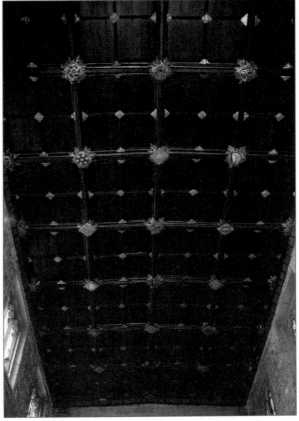

The painted oak ceiling at All Hallows, Almondbury.

At the west end of the nave below the tower is the baptistery; the beautiful font cover is Tudor in date, and was restored in 1936.

For Almondbury take the A642 (Wakefield) from Huddersfield
There are several right lanes to Almondbury, but the preferred route is to fork right at the A642/A629 junction
On the A629 (Sheffield) in ¾ mile turn right at the Star Inn
Follow Fenay Lane to Almondbury

Or   Penistone Line to Huddersfield
At the bus station, take bus service 341 and 342 for Almondbury

Lockwood, Huddersfield: Beaumont Park and the Beaumonts

If you join the Sheffield-bound train at Huddersfield you will hardly have settled into your seat and passed through the tunnel before the train slows down for the first stop on the Penistone Line at Lockwood.

From here a short walk (uphill) will take you to the first of Huddersfield's parks; its 20 acres known locally as Dungeon Wood were donated to the town by Mr H.F. Beaumont in 1879. There were several branches of the Beaumont family; their local estate was at Whitley Beaumont near Kirkheaton.

Such was the excitement in Huddersfield about the gift of land to allow for the creation of a public park that only a Royal opening would do, and on 13 October 1883 the Duke and Duchess of Albany performed the ceremony. The Duke was the youngest son of Queen Victoria, his wife being Princess Helena Fredericka Augusta, who planted a tree. The Duke opened the park gates with a golden key carrying his coat of arms and that of Mr H.F. Beaumont. There was a grand procession from town, led by local brass bands, and after the ceremony the Royal visitors received hospitality from the Beaumonts at Whitley Beaumont.

Work on developing the park had gone on for the previous three years, exploiting its unusual features. The upper area, which is narrow and flat, was landscaped, planted and given a Main Walk with seats and a bandstand. Below is a steep, often precipitous slope: above and beyond the trees are wonderful glimpses of distant views, including the Penistone Line viaduct in the valley.

Beaumont Park, Lockwood.

Castle Hill and railway viaduct from Beaumont Park.

A network of paths and steps was built into the hillside to allow visitors to see the woods and the wildlife that abounds there. It is something of a wilderness park below the quarry-like rocky cliffs that provide shelter and encourage plant growth.

Over the years there have been several changes in the park and the steady growth of trees and bushes has created a need for conservation work. On the steep slopes, care has been taken not to cause the loss of soil when roots have had to be removed.

The park has always been a popular and valuable amenity, particularly for the Lockwood and Crosland Moor area of Huddersfield, but soon after Beaumont Park was opened, Greenhead Park near the centre of Huddersfield, with sports facilities and conservatories, started to develop (see p. 32). This left Beaumont Park to the Lockwood locals and nature lovers. If you like peace and quiet, Beaumont Park is the place to be.

If you are interested in the Beaumont family, go the short distance to see St John's Church at Kirkheaton. Fragments of an Anglo-Saxon cross have been found on the site, suggesting that there was a stone church before the Conquest. Until 1200, Kirkheaton was just a part of the Dewsbury parish; at that date Kirkheaton became a parish in its own right and a large church was built.

We know that Beaumont money went into that medieval church, as in Henry Beaumont's will dated 1468, there are bequests towards the tower and to hanging the bells. Most of that early church has now gone, resulting from a major re-building programme in 1823 and another re-build following a serious fire in 1886. Today, only the tower and the Beaumont Chapel remain of the medieval church, but they are, of course, of great interest.

The Beaumont Chapel was, originally, a chantry dedicated to the Blessed Virgin Mary; such chantries were built to ensure that prayers were regularly said for the souls of the departed. When these chantries were abolished in the sixteenth century, the Beaumonts took the chantry as a private chapel, having used it for many years as a family burial place. As far back as 1574 Edward Beaumont asked to be buried in his 'own' chapel there; at about that time the chapel was extended eastwards.

The earliest monument is a brass to Adam Beaumont (who died in 1615) and his wife, but the tomb of Sir Richard Beaumont ('Black Dick') who died in 1631 always excites visitors because of its fine painting and its elaborate canopy. He had quite a reputation! Allow plenty of time for the chapel and the rest of the church.

But that is not all; at the church gate is a poignant reminder of the children who worked in the local mills; in 1818 a factory fire at Colne Bridge nearby killed seventeen children, all girls. The monument is in their memory.

Just across from the church gate is the Beaumont Arms, known locally as Kirkstile. Parishioners could take refreshment there after Sunday services before

St John's Church, Kirkheaton.

their long journeys home across the large parish. There were stables at Kirkstile for churchgoers to leave their horses and the churchwardens held their meetings there. Apparently their drinks were at the public expense and there were many attempts to limit the quantity of drink consumed!

Sadly, the great house of the Beaumont family, Whitley Beaumont, was demolished in 1952; earlier, in 1948, the male line of the Beaumonts ended with the death of Henry Ralph, son of the donor of Dungeon Wood, H.F. Beaumont.

There are architectural accounts of Whitley Beaumont, but I like the children's story about it, the 'Whitley Marble'. As a schoolboy from Staincliffe, Brian Tattersfield first saw the house during a long car journey; it was uninhabited, ruined and in course of demolition. He was fascinated by it and recorded its rooms before it disappeared altogether, producing a book written and illustrated by his wife Mary. It tells the story of Will, whose favourite marble had magical properties and showed him a huge house (Whitley Beaumont?) he knew well.

The tomb of Sir Richard Beaumont in Kirkheaton Church.

For Lockwood take the A616 from Huddersfield to Lockwood traffic lights
Continue towards Meltham, turn right uphill to park
Kerbside parking can be found opposite the park

Or   Penistone Line to Lockwood
From the station follow Bentley Street to Meltham Road
Fork right on to Beaumont Park Road

For Kirkheaton take the A642 from Huddersfield (Wakefield)
At the A629 junction keep left, then turn left immediately
After ½ mile at the T-junction turn right up the hill
On the right is Church Lane (the Beaumont Arms sign is on the corner)

Or   Penistone Line to Huddersfield
Bus service 317 to Kirkheaton
Service runs every 30 minutes. Journey time: 15 minutes

The Penistone Line &
Holme Valley Stations

Hardly have Penistone Line trains left Huddersfield station and emerged from the tunnel than they turn south away from the tracks carrying the Manchester-bound services along the Colne Valley. Penistone Line trains make for the Holme Valley, a fascinating short section of the line that, unusually, follows the contours of the map. There are only four stations on this early part of the route, even counting Lockwood which is part of Huddersfield.

By the time the trains reach the next station, Berry Brow, where walkers can go to Castle Hill, the tracks are following the river and the road. They remain in the Holme Valley for a brief 15 minutes after leaving Huddersfield.

Streams have always run down the valley sides, draining the high moorland and watering the meadows below; farming and cottage spinning and weaving formed the pattern of life in this rolling countryside until the Industrial Revolution changed everything. There had always been soft water for washing wool; the first mills used waterpower, followed by steam, and this created a massive textile industry. It is said that up to 60 textile mills operated in the once rural Holme valley.

Now the mills have closed or are used for other purposes, though the valley's industrial heritage can still be seen, along with its fine rural landscape. So attractive is it that the Holme Valley Riverside Way has been created especially for walkers. It starts at Steps Bridge at the bottom of Magdale and finishes at Digley Reservoir near Holme.

The total distance covered is 6 miles, but the route has been carefully divided into four sections that provide comfortable shorter walks.

Holme Valley stations: Honley

Honley has a long history; its name means 'dwelling in a clearing' and there is evidence of an early settlement by the Brigantes, later to be subdued by the Romans. In 1893 an important collection of Roman coins was discovered, perhaps buried for safety reasons, which became known as the Honley 'find'.

Honley's main street, Westgate, rises up steeply from the valley bottom; beyond the town westward is Honley Moor at an elevation of over 1,000ft. The River Holme and its tributary Mag Brook have always been a valuable resource for industry. Even today, industry at Honley is concentrated near these waterways – such as at Steps Industrial Park.

Honley station on the Penistone Line is inconveniently located uphill on the east of the river; to reach it from the centre of Honley means going first downhill to the crossroads. Since Honley is a road junction for Sheffield and for Holmfirth, it is a busy crossing, something of a barrier as far as the Penistone Line is concerned. It is ironic to see that alongside the station is an extensive bus park.

The parish church of St Mary stands prominently to the north of the town; Church Street and the little streets and folds round it are old, narrow and paved with setts. For the most picturesque, look for France Fold, Doctor Fold and New Street; the parish stocks can be seen near the church door.

St Mary's Church.

France Fold.

49

William Leighton's house.

The Coach & Horses pub.

In St Mary's Square stands the oldest house in Honley, and almost directly opposite the church is Leighton House, very much part of the town's industrial history. William Leighton was an affluent textile manufacturer, but in spite of his generosity to the town, his house was attacked in 1817 during the violence associated with the so-called Folly Hall riots that were an extension of the Luddite activities of 1812. (For more information on this see *Yorkshire's Historic Pubs*, Peter Thomas, Sutton Publishing.)

In the Coach & Horses public house, close to Honley Bridge, are two reports of the murder of William Horsfall, a well-known mill owner, who was attacked on Crosland Moor. Witnesses agreed that four men were involved and the pub landlady at the time, Mrs Robinson, giving evidence at their York trial, claimed that she had seen two young men at the pub that day. Although there seems to have been no positive identification of the men who killed Horsfall, and they claimed to have had alibis, they were convicted and executed. Prominent in the search for the culprits and other Luddite supporters was Joseph Radcliffe, a magistrate and landowner of Milnsbridge House; a picture of him is at the head of the main report.

A gem of Honley's early industrial history is just off the main Huddersfield/ New Mill road at the sign 'Steps Industrial Park'. Cross the river bridge and turn left away from the industrial site and follow the public right of way to the point where Mag Brook passes over a weir before joining the River Holme. Close to a little bridge is the millpool; beyond it is the former Upper Steps Mill. On a calm day its reflection in the water is superb. It was, of course, powered by a waterwheel; remains of its housing are visible.

Upper Steps Mill reflected in the Mill Pool.

Brockholes

In the Village Hall, formerly the school, is a large banner proclaiming the Badger Youth Club: Brock was the Anglo-Saxon word for Badger and Holes means hollow. Hence Brockholes.

Smaller than Honley and 'only an engine whistle away' on the opposite side of the valley, Brockholes was of importance on the Penistone Line as the junction for Holmfirth, close to the entrance to the Thurstonland Tunnel that led on to Stocksmoor and Shepley out of the Holme valley.

Part of the village is scattered along the A616 New Mill road, but the village centre is further east between the A616 and the railway. Like other villages in the area, past employment was largely in farming or textiles – sometimes both; life was hard, forcing people to dig for coal from hillside 'day holes'. For some years there was quarrying at Robin Rocks, but today work is found elsewhere and commuting is a way of modern life.

Rock outcrops are typical of the hillside scenery here, one feature being known as Tor Rocks. The Rock Inn took its name from the high jagged rocks that thrust out over the main road; from the pub car park the church can be seen in a remarkable location. Rock Mills, established in 1870, also took its name from the scenery. Owned by Joseph Sykes, it was one of the largest mills in the area, employing over 500 people; unusually, it carried out all the processes from scouring raw wool to the production of worsted cloth. It was demolished in 1975.

A train at Brockholes Junction, 1958. (P. Sunderland)

The Rock Inn.

Rocks at Brockholes. The church can just be seen behind the trees.

Brockholes was dependent on its larger neighbour, Honley, for many things including its parish church. Then, in 1861, St George's was built on the rocks through the generosity of Miss Marianne Armitage; her family came from Armitage Bridge, from which they took their name.

It is said that Miss Armitage once saw some children outside the Honley Sunday School, wet through, having walked from Brockholes in the rain. She

St George's Church.

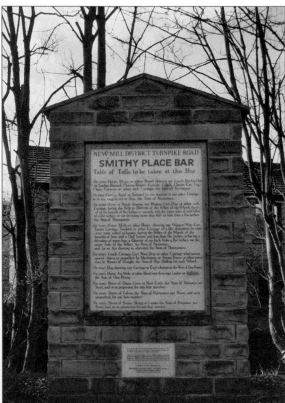

Smithy Place Bar, where turnpike tolls were collected.

determined that Brockholes should have its own church. She is on record as supporting a number of churches in addition to that at Brockholes.

The Brookes were another leading family. They founded a textile mill in the early eighteenth century; John Brooke seems to have been a progressive businessman and was quick to replace waterwheels with steam power at his mill.

A pleasant walk is up Oakes Lane at Brockholes. A path across fields leads to the railway line close to the tunnel entrance; this was the notorious Thurstonland Tunnel where the first train on the line's opening day came to grief (see p. 6).

At the top of Oakes Lane, Birch Park leads off to the left; the houses here were built on the embankment of the former branch line from Brockholes to Holmfirth.

Stocksmoor to Shepley

Station to station and pub to pub: a gentle walk

One look at the Penistone Line timetable shows how close in proximity the stations are to each other: a mere three minute journey apart. In such attractive surroundings a gentle half hour's walk is a wonderful way to unwind: to have excellent pubs at each end as well is a real bonus.

The name Shepley hardly needs explanation. Yes, this is sheep country with plenty of footpaths. The landlady at Stocksmoor's Clothiers' agreed to walk and time it for me. I am sure she will have 'stepped out', but even so we agreed on half an hour from village to village.

Stocksmoor station and the Clothiers' Arms next door.

Stocksmoor: The Clothiers' Arms

Having made my first visit to the Clothiers' Arms at Stocksmoor by a Penistone Line train, I walked right from the platform to the pub car park. It couldn't be nearer or more convenient!

When I saw the pub sign on my next visit I was intrigued. It shows a person (man or woman), a huge pair of scissors, a roll of cloth, reels of thread, a measuring tape and a pin cushion. *That's* a tailor I said, *not* a clothier. He was, in the old days, a supplier of yarn to cottage weavers and a merchant who would market the finished products. Gilbert and Sullivan would have had fun with this and surely have called it 'a most ingenious paradox'. Remember Frederick in *The Pirates of Penzance*? He was born on 29 February in a Leap Year and had lived 21 years, yet was 'only five and a little bit over'. It really doesn't matter, of course, if the pub is a good one – and it is.

Until the mid-1880s the pub was called the New Inn; it was taken over by two textile manufacturers at that time, which probably explains the change of name to Clothiers' Arms. Local belief is that the cloth makers' guild used to meet here. The building itself dates from the eighteenth century, so it could have been a beer house and farm with an even earlier name than the New Inn. There

The pub sign of the Clothiers' Arms.

are some handsome former weavers' cottages on Cross Lane near to the road to Thurstonland as evidence of an early domestic textile industry at Stocksmoor; no shortage of wool, either, judging by the sheep grazing here!

In the nineteenth century the Clothiers' Arms became one of Seth Senior's 140 pubs; his brewery was a major business in Shepley.

There are two anecdotes worth telling about Stocksmoor and the Clothier's Arms. One concerned two engineers sent to Stocksmoor where a Penistone Line train was stranded in a snowdrift. At the pub they saw this *very* fat lady and discussed whether they would be able to join hands round her girth. We don't know whether a bet was made, but the lady must have cooperated. It is understood that the engineers were able to 'touch fingers'.

The other is a legendary account of a day when a television crew was in the area years ago filming *Last of the Summer Wine* and saw a workman at the station coal yard wearing an appalling jacket. Thinking that it would be just the thing for Compo, they bought it for £5; you will remember that he wore it in some style, tied up with string.

You will find the Clothiers' Arms warm, comfortable and welcoming: in fact, just the place to set off on a country walk. Ring Suzy on 01484 602752 to check opening hours and don't forget to look at the pub sign.

The Walk

From the Clothiers' Arms turn right to the junction of Stocks Moor Road and Birks Lane. Turn right downhill on Birks Lane, through the woods (pavement all the way) to Thunderbridge; at the crossroads turn right on Dam Hill. After about

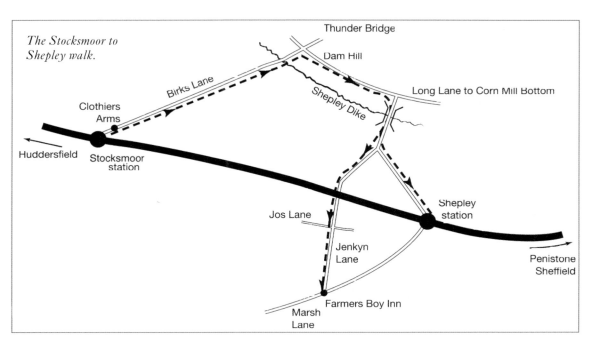

The Stocksmoor to Shepley walk.

Stocksmoor to Shepley: turn into Long Lane, then pass over the stone bridge.

400 yards a road sign names a public right of way – Long Lane – leading right to Corn Mill Bottom. Follow it and cross Shepley Dike by a footbridge; climb the slope beyond along a walled path through a gate to a path crossing a field. A left-hand fork is a more direct route to Shepley station; a right-hand fork leads uphill to Jos Lane/Wood Lane. Cross into Jenkyn Lane and continue towards Marsh Lane. The Farmer's Boy is on the corner of Jenkyn Lane and Marsh Lane.

Shepley: The Farmer's Boy and Old Barn Restaurant

Shepley was once quite a place for breweries: Highfield (Seth Senior), Cliffe Top (Joseph Bentley) and Sovereign (Thomas M. Carter). All of them were founded in the nineteenth century with Seth Senior being the oldest and largest; Senior's produced 1,000 barrels of beer a week.

Seth Senior's brewery continued to operate until 1946, when it was taken over by Hammond's Brewery of Lockwood near Huddersfield. It is believed locally that Seth borrowed a sovereign to start brewing in his own cottage which led him to advertise his product as Sovereign Ales.

In the 1880s eight pubs were listed in Shepley, including the Farmer's Boy; licensees there included Joseph Addy (1838) and David Addy, his son (1868). It was a beer house then and may have brewed its own beer, at least until Seth Senior set up his brewery in 1829; the pub was also a farm, working 32 acres of land. Without any doubt the Farmer's Boy and neighbouring cottages had weavers upstairs; a look at the enlarged windows will confirm that. The Old Barn Restaurant is on the site of the main barn at the back of the farmhouse and pub.

In those early days Marsh Lane was an important highway and the Farmer's Boy would have been a coaching inn on it; further up Marsh Lane from Shepley village a right-hand fork led into Long Close Lane. Although this appears a minor track, it swings in a wide curve until taking a westerly direction only yards short

The Farmer's Boy at Shepley: once a coaching inn and now renowned for good food.

The Old Barn at the Farmer's Boy with Ruth behind the bar.

of the modern A635 road and follows its line to New Mill, then all points north and west. We can picture coaches using this route before anyone dreamed of the need to build the A635 as it is today.

The land on which the Farmer's Boy stands was once part of the Radcliffe estate based on Milnsbridge House in the Colne valley. The pub itself changed hands several times, twentieth-century breweries like Charringtons and Bass selling it on in turn. The bar is traditional with small rooms, in contrast to the Old Barn which is open plan and rustic in atmosphere.

There have been plenty of reported 'presences' felt in the Farmer's Boy. Male presences have been felt many times; they have never done harm, but are quite real to the licensees, their family and employees. The ghost of a kindly lady in a long dress has appeared in the past to several people, including a young girl in bed who saw the lady tucking in the bedclothes. She never slept in the bed again and alterations to the bedrooms seem to have ended the appearances upstairs.

Whatever spectres from the past may have appeared in the Old Barn, which has seen most of the unexplained events, I have never had the pleasure and have always enjoyed an uninterrupted steak and ale pie.

Although the walk from Stocksmoor Clothiers' Arms to Shepley Farmer's Boy has also been recommended as a Penistone Line station to station walk, there are other possibilities. You may have a member of your group who is not a great walker and who would rather read his paper, order the drinks and meet you with the car. If so, get him to buy lunch at the Old Barn. When planning your walk ring Janet on 01484 605941 for opening hours and meal times.

To reach Shepley station from the Farmer's Boy turn left out of the pub and walk down Marsh Lane past the library to the crossroads, then turn left into Station Road.

For Stocksmoor (start of the walk) take the A629/642 from Huddersfield to the junction at Waterloo
Keep right on the A629 past Kirkburton
Fork right for Thunderbridge and Stocksmoor
Pass Woodman Inn and after ½ mile turn left

Or   Penistone Line to Stocksmoor

Denby Dale

When the Penistone Line train reaches Denby Dale you have a bonus: a bird's-eye view of the whole town as you cross the enormous viaduct which crosses the main street and the River Dearne. Of course, you see little of the viaduct itself from the train; that is something to wonder at from ground level. Its 21 arches dwarf everything around it. It was originally built of wood on grounds of cost, but the risk it presented led to its replacement in stone in 1880.

Both river and railway were of great importance for Denby Dale, which until the early nineteenth century was known as Denby Dyke. Like so many of the

Denby Dale: some of the great arches of the railway viaduct.

Denby Dale Pie Hall, opened in 1972.

Yorkshire villages by streams or rivers, Denby Dale's main work was in textiles. What began as a domestic industry changed to factory production as new inventions made it more profitable. Waterwheels producing power from the rivers served the first mills; the coming of the railway from Huddersfield to Penistone in 1850 led to further development of textile manufacturing through the use of steam to drive machinery.

At one time three mills were working at Denby Dale, but the only visible sign of those days is the great Springfield Mill just off Wakefield Road, a short distance from the viaduct. Today, a wide range of retail businesses occupy the building and attract many visitors; a restaurant on the ground floor is recommended – especially its meat and potato pie!

Beyond the shops on Wakefield Road is the branch library and, almost opposite, the Pie Hall which was opened in 1972 as a village hall. Outside it is a remarkable flowerbed contained in the dish of a massive Denby Dale pie made in 1964 and weighing six tons; the sale of portions of the pie raised enough to build the Pie Hall.

The dish which contained the 1964 pie, Denby Dale.

If for nothing else, Denby Dale is remembered for its huge pies and the ten occasions (the last being the Millennium, when the pie weighed 12.52 tonnes) that important events like the defeat of Napoleon at Waterloo were celebrated in the town.

Pie size will certainly continue to be an essential feature of the Denby Dale tradition; Barnsley is only about eight miles away and strong local loyalties would not want Denby Dale pies to be upstaged by the traditional Barnsley Chop!

Although the A636 Wakefield road passes through the centre of Denby Dale, a road junction just west of the viaduct provides a turning to the A635 Barnsley road; further west still, beyond Cumberworth, are crossroads where the Manchester-bound A636 crosses the A629 route from Huddersfield to Sheffield (also to junction 36 of the M1).

The Penistone Line offers an hourly service in both directions from Denby Dale: north to Huddersfield and south to Penistone, Barnsley and Sheffield.

Clayton West: The Kirklees Light Railway

After the closure of the Clayton West branch line in 1983, Kirklees Council planned to buy the track bed and were minded to landscape the area previously used by the railway and the collieries.

This would have gone forward but for a request by Brian Taylor in 1990 for a lease of the track bed for the building of a 15-inch gauge railway. He had built a number of steam locomotives which he proposed to use to carry passengers on the line.

After many difficulties he was successful and track laying by the Kirklees Light Railway Co. began. On 19 October 1991 the first steam train ran on a 1 mile route from Clayton West to Cuckoo's Nest. Today the line has reached Shelley, 4 miles from the Clayton West base where there is an engine shed and a turntable; the former station building and site have been developed as a visitor centre.

It was one of those magical moments. I was getting into my car at the Pennine Nurseries at Shelley when I noticed a moving trail of smoke in the valley below – and was that a train whistle? Yes, it was, and from then on I was hooked. It is said that boys of all ages are affected this way – just watch boys and their fathers crowding round to see the engines being turned round on the turntables at Clayton West and Shelley.

The turntable at Shelley on the Kirklees Light Railway.

All aboard at Clayton West!

Shortly before Christmas 2005, Graham Hurd entertained guests at Clayton West to celebrate taking over the railway, and it soon became clear that there was a new hand on the 'regulator', to use engine-driver speak. Graham's energy and enthusiasm shines through; he plans to redevelop the Clayton West station building, where there is already a spacious restaurant and shop. But he also wants passengers to enjoy Shelley as a destination, not just a turn round point. The return journey takes 50 minutes, but Graham hopes people will stay at Shelley and Clayton West and make a day of it.

One of the signs his ideas are taking shape is the big poster display in the restaurant that illustrates the development on and around the line. BBC2's Christine Walkden's six-month horticultural project already shows results. On the facing platform are masses of container flowers, the work of local volunteers. More volunteer work is needed in a whole variety of activities.

School holidays bring an influx of visitors, particularly for Thomas and Friends, but there is always plenty to do and see: the café and shop, loco shed visits, picnic sites and country walks. The miniature railway that runs round the pond between the car park and station building is very popular. The Kirklees Light Railway also hosts children's parties.

For your journey to Shelley and back, expect to have steam engines Fox (red) or Badger (green) in charge. Hawk is blue and a bigger engine, used for special work such as footplate experience days. If you have always wanted to drive a steam locomotive (go on, confess!) you can at Clayton West.

Graham's 2006 event list makes exciting reading: the Easter Eggspress, a day out with Thomas, Wild West Weekend, Teddy Bear's Picnic, Halloween Ghost Train and Santa Specials.

You may, like me, just want to enjoy the journey. The scenery is superb, passing Cuckoo's Nest, Blacker Wood, with Emley television mast keeping company so close that it hardly seems possible. A whistle and a 5mph approach warn of Skelmanthorpe ahead. There are fields with grazing cattle, rocky cuttings with ferns and trees. It's all there, including the 511-yard long Shelley Woodhouse Tunnel – when the carriage lights come on – before braking gently into Shelley station. The re-surfaced platform has transformed its appearance and Graham plans a drinks/ice cream vending machine there.

The Kirklees Light Railway is open every weekend throughout the year, and every day from the end of May to early September and all school holidays. Trains run every hour from 11 a.m.

> For Clayton West take junction 38 off the M1 then the A637 towards
> Huddersfield
> Pass Yorkshire Sculpture Park and West Bretton
> At the next roundabout take the A636 towards Denby Dale
> At Clayton West turn left after the railway bridge

> Or   Penistone Line: From Denby Dale, rural bus service 935
> Hourly service. Journey time: 5 minutes
> At Clayton West, Wakefield Road, opposite Albert Road

Clayton West: Kirklees Light Railway – the Footplate Experience

The café at the station's Visitor Centre was busy; most of the tables were occupied at 12.30 p.m. with passengers waiting for the next train. Over in the far corner a chorus of children's voices began singing 'Happy Birthday to You'.

By the engine shed stood *Badger*, steaming quietly, her green livery lovingly polished by Matthew, today's driver and instructor who was waiting for his next trainee driver: me. *Badger*'s saddle tanks make her easily recognisable, her small wheels give her extra power on the gradient towards Skelmanthorpe, our destination for today's footplate experience.

While the 1 p.m. train at platform 1 was loading, we topped up with water at the water column; *Badger* would use half of her water capacity on the afternoon's run and filling up to the top would give us a safety margin. Matthew added a measure of chemical to remove impurities that might damage *Badger*; six shovels full of coal went into the firebox. Oil in all the lubrication points, an inspection all round and we were ready to go. We needed to be in Skelmanthorpe by 1.35 p.m. to allow the passenger train returning from Shelley to pass us there at 1.40 p.m. It had now left Clayton West on the outward run, so the track was clear.

Matthew took the left-hand seat to demonstrate the controls and showed me which dials to watch. He checked for forward move, released the brake and opened the regulator slightly and carefully. 'You will think nothing is happening at first, just be patient'. We moved off, gathering a little speed as we passed curious onlookers sitting on platform seats. Of course, we did not have a train behind us, so no doubt we looked odd.

We passed the signals on the bridge over the road and began to pick up speed; ahead the track stretched out clearly towards distant trees. *Badger*'s narrow wheel base dealt comfortably with the little irregularities in the track and soon we saw a red light; the company's tractor, where sleeper-laying was going on.

Matthew whistled, eased the regulator and we went on slowly with plenty of clearance for the tractor as we passed. Now *Badger* started to use her power to deal with the long gradient, a steady engine rhythm, Emley television mast always close by on the right. An unexpected long whistle: Matthew had seen a grouse on the line and it found frightened refuge in a trackside bush. 'Those are badger setts on the right', he told me.

We whistled for two 'occupational' unmanned level crossings and approached the bridge at Skelmanthorpe station. Slowly now, a limit of 5mph for the points here and Matthew set them for us to go on to the loop so that the returning passenger train from Shelley could pass us. The collieries have long since gone here and their railway business with them; replacing them are anonymous industrial buildings which occupy the land and rely on road transport. We take photographs, note the distance sign – 1¾ miles to Clayton West – and look at the former arrangements for passengers crossing the bridge and descending stone steps to join the trains at Skelmanthorpe.

Right on time the returning train moved slowly past us towards Clayton West; more curious faces looking at *Badger* and at us. Now we changed seats and I was

The author driving Badger *at Skelmanthorpe.*

sitting at the regulator doing the necessary checks. 'Take her forward slowly beyond the points' said Matthew and, rather hesitantly, we moved and I applied the brake. 'Just a little further', so we did it again, a little more confidently this time. Matthew set the points and said 'Now take her back to Cuckoo's Nest'. There is no turntable at Skelmanthorpe, so we would be in reverse: I wound on the control for reverse and eased the regulator. Much to my surprise, *Badger* did exactly what I wanted, Matthew watching every move and adding to my peace of mind by saying he would take the engine back home from Cuckoo's Nest.

It was a challenge, regulating speed, stopping exactly when and where required and watching the track ahead at all times. But, of course, there are no irresponsible drivers as there are on the roads, no bewildering (and sometimes contradictory) road signs and no danger of taking a wrong turning.

Driving tender first, as they say in the trade, seems to add to engine speed as the track races away to the rear. We were, of course, on a downhill gradient of at least 1 in 70. A car-type driving mirror would be of little help: its vision is limited and I would want to be all-seeing, especially when trying to judge distance and to be ready for the next move to make.

It is said that boys of all ages want to drive a steam locomotive – now I know why. Until you have tried it you will not know the experience you have missed.

High Flatts (Quaker Bottom) and Bullhouse Chapel

Since Queen Elizabeth's death in 1603, followed by the Stuart dynasty, people had become critical of the established Church and dissenters had formed groups to worship together. Meetings for worship were the focus of their lives, but many group members felt the need to meet socially and to provide mutual support.

Until 1689, nonconformist religious meetings were against the law and fear of punishment led groups like the Quakers to seek remote places for worship. High Flatts was one of these places, although early meetings often took place in the open air, in members' houses or farm buildings: anywhere that did not draw attention to the dissent being practised. In the course of time, the larger and more active groups built their Meeting Houses when persecution ceased; Wooldale, near Holmfirth was, like High Flatts, a strong group and both went on to build their own Meeting House. Support increasingly came from wealthy business families such as the Jacksons of Totties Hall. They were clothiers and it was Henry Jackson who built a bridge en route between his properties at Totties and Meal Hill; it became known as Jackson's Bridge and the village there is now Jackson Bridge.

Quakers at High Flatts met for worship in a barn for many years, but by 1750 they had their own Meeting House – plain inside with benches, a table and a Bible. For a long time Wooldale was under the authority of High Flatts, but later became independent. By the mid-eighteenth century the Quakers were the largest group of Dissenters in Yorkshire; the congregations at High Flatts, joined by people from other parishes, were up to 100.

At the little hamlet of High Flatts on the Barnsley road, opposite Windmill Lane, a quiet cobbled road leads downhill to a cluster of stone buildings; further, in the distance, today's Penistone Line snakes its way in a huge curve towards

The Friends' Meeting House at High Flatts.

Penistone. Denby Dale is down there, the only township anywhere near. Life here in the country was apparently very peaceful in the eighteenth century.

Over the years improvements to the Meeting House at High Flatts were made, although the interior remained plain and utilitarian; an extension to the burial ground was necessary too and can be visited behind the Meeting House. High Flatts was essentially a Quaker community mainly occupied in wool textiles, although some did farm work; a few did both.

The striking feature of the dwellings clustered closely round a courtyard near the Meeting House is the neighbourliness of those who lived there. They were dependent on the outside world for their livelihood, but shared the beliefs of the members around them. Their principle of caring for others is well-established. They opened a day school at High Flatts in the eighteenth century and some of the Friends undertook teaching themselves. Further afield, they founded a village school at Birdsedge; the Quaker school at Ackworth is nationally known.

There were problems, of course: from the late eighteenth century there was a movement of members away from High Flatts to take mill work in Huddersfield and Sheffield. Together with a fall in membership at that time, the future at High Flatts began to look bleak, but there was a slow recovery, particularly at High Flatts compared with elsewhere. The community there showed itself as being special; it is impossible not to be inspired both by the Quakers' strength of faith and by the relationship they had with each other and the place they called home – High Flatts.

The Quaker burial ground and Friends' houses.

Today's community is varied and residential, but the Quaker meetings continue as they have done for over 300 years.

For High Flatts take the A629 from Huddersfield turn just after Birdsedge

Or *Penistone Line to Huddersfield*
    From Huddersfield (Lord Street). Bus service 237
    Infrequent service. Journey time: 30 minutes

71

Penistone

Millstone Green, near Penistone: Bullhouse Chapel

Religious disagreement which was a feature of the Civil War continued to divide the country afterwards. Areas that had been strongly Puritan remained so, strengthened by the beliefs of leading families in whose gift was often the presentation of living to clergy. Of these the Rich family were prominent landowners in the Thurlstone, Millhouse and Bullhouse areas and were prepared to support the vicar of Penistone, Henry Swift, who refused to conform to the Act of Uniformity and was in danger of being ejected from his living in the 1660s. Although he refused to wear a surplice and to use the recognised Prayer Book, they gave him protection; he remained in office until he died in 1689.

Bullhouse Chapel and former minister's cottage, Millstone Green.

The interior of Bullhouse Chapel.

The right to present the living at Penistone was in question on his death and the Crown appointed a vicar with the 'correct' credentials. The Toleration Act of 1672 had already given some relief to nonconformists and Sylvanus Rich licensed his home, Bullhouse Hall as a meeting place. Sylvanus died in 1683 and was succeeded by his son Elkanah, who was able to take advantage of a second Toleration Act in 1689 to have legally recognised meetings at his house.

In 1692, Elkanah had the Bullhouse Chapel built on his own land, only a stone's throw from the Hall. He appointed and paid for a minister, who was granted a tiny cottage attached to the chapel; the cottage now serves as vestry for the chapel. In those early days a congregation of 200 was recorded; today's membership is much smaller, but the congregation are proud of the chapel's Independent status and its being the oldest building in the county with a continuous history of nonconformist worship.

In 1825 a Sunday school was opened and from 1843 the minister ran a day school for the children of poor families in the chapel; this continued until 1878 when Millhouse School was built. Since 1926, there has been an annual performance of Handel's *Messiah* in the chapel, an event which fills the chapel once again.

The chapel is close to a working farm as well as Bullhouse Hall at the end of narrow Bullhouse Lane, about 400 yards from the A628 Manchester road. Below

The matchstick model of Bullhouse Chapel.

the chapel, in a deep cutting, the Trans Pennine Trail follows the track bed of the railway that ran from the Yorkshire coalfields through Penistone and the Woodhead Tunnel into Lancashire. This explains why the chapel's sandstone walls are soot-blackened. The only exterior decorations are the four ball finials resembling those on the Hall; the central door is also plain.

On entering, plain pews are on the left and to the right is the chief feature, the original pulpit set high and with a sounding canopy. The walls have plain panelling, with a row of hat pegs, and there is plenty of light. A recent addition to the interior is a model of the chapel made entirely from matchsticks. It stands close to the vestry door – do not miss this exhibit.

Please remember that the chapel is on private property, which visitors are asked to respect. Bullhouse Lane has numerous 'No Parking' notices, but there is limited parking space to be found by the entrance to the chapel grounds.

For further information contact the Secretary on: 01226 763353.

> *For Bullhouse Chapel take junction 37 off the M1 then the A628 via Penistone and Millstone Green*
> *Turn right at the Millennium Bridge*

> *Or   Penistone Line to Penistone*
> *Bus service 24 to Bullhouse Lane*
> *Infrequent service. Journey time: 15 minutes*

Penistone: Parish Church of St John the Baptist

The parish church of St John the Baptist in Penistone is open to the public on Thursdays from 10 a.m. to 12 noon. Its 80ft-tower is a landmark for miles and better than any signpost to the centre of the town. It probably dates from about 1500 and is decorated with pinnacles; the nave roof is embattled and pinnacled too, but the chancel roof line is plain.

Both nave and chancel were built in about 1200, but various changes and extensions were carried out over the centuries, the present tower being the latest addition. A first impression of the nave is that the builders were reluctant to abandon building the massive round piers so familiar at Durham Cathedral in favour of a more decorative octagonal shape; here at Penistone, both forms have been used alternately.

The porch came much later, in the eighteenth century, using stones taken from the remains of a medieval chapel dedicated to St John the Baptist in Chapel Lane. Such separate chapels were often tended by a custodian or priest; they provided for regular prayers on behalf of the souls of the departed, usually members of prominent families who gave land and money for the upkeep of the chantries, as they were called.

The parish church of St John the Baptist.

The font at Penistone parish church.

The carved oak roof.

Two chantry chapels were built within the church: on the north of the chancel was that of St Erasmus and St Anthony, now the vestry, and close to the chancel arch on the south side was the Lady Chapel. This served as a Chantry School in 1392; it can be said to be the origin of Penistone Grammar School.

Across the church the chancel pillar on the north side contains a stone that was once part of an Anglo-Saxon cross, apparently useful to the Norman church builders. Ancient too, is the massive stone that forms the top of the altar and the font in the baptistery below the tower.

Most celebrated of all the church's interior features are the 43 carvings on the oak roof; 31 of them are decorated bosses where the ribs of the roof meet, 12 being corbels where the roof supports are attached to the wall.

Flowers such as marigolds can be identified, also varieties of foliage; one head is thought to be that of John the Baptist. The corbels are mainly portraits, including the mother and father of John the Baptist, and a nobleman believed to be John of Gaunt; he later became Duke of Lancaster and Lord of Penistone.

To the east of the church is a recently completed curved stone pathway with decorative bays. It is a piece of imaginative landscaping leading from Shrewsbury Road to Church Street opposite to the Community Centre. At intervals along the pathway are commemorative stones recording major dates in the town's history:

A train traversing Penistone viaduct. (B. Barnsley)

c. 1000	Saxon Cross in St John's Church
1086	Pengeston recorded in the Domesday Book
1120	Penistone becomes an independent parish
1392	Penistone Grammar School founded
1500	St John's Church tower built
1699	Penistone Thursday Market Charter granted
1783	Penistone Cloth Hall built
1850	Penistone's 29 arch viaduct completed
1863	First steelworks built in Penistone
1913	Carnegie Free Library built

For Penistone church take junction 37 off the M1 then follow the A628 towards Manchester
At Penistone traffic lights follow signs for the town centre
Keep left on St Mary's Street then into Church Street

Or   Penistone Line to Penistone
Walk downhill and under the bridge
At the crossroads keep left on Shrewsbury Road
Pass the Paramount Cinema
The church is on the right

Penistone: The Paramount Cinema and its Compton Organ

With acknowledgement to Kevin Grunill & the Penistone Organ Trust

There are no prizes for this. What do the following names mean to you: Sydney Torch, Reginald Porter-Brown, Robin Richmond and Sandy Macpherson? Anything? If nothing then let me add Reginald Dixon – they are, of course, a reminder of the great days of cinema and theatre organs. In those days a visit to the cinema was exciting – even more so if a mighty, glittering Compton or Wurlitzer organ arose as if by magic from below the stage with the organist playing his signature tune.

Reg Dixon will always be associated with the Tower Ballroom, Blackpool, but sadly, once the great cinemas of the 1930s fell out of favour, the organs they housed lost a home and the organists who played there were only remembered by lovers of organ music. Today few organs are left; but the story of the Compton and the Paramount Cinema in Penistone is one with a happy ending, and a tribute to one man – Kevin Grunill, Resident Team Organist today based at the Tower Ballroom, Blackpool.

Kevin's ambition was to acquire an organ with the right sound and to find a home for it. The result is that Penistone has the only fully working cinema/theatre in the north of England and Scotland to house a British-built Compton Cinema organ – and what an atmosphere it has!

As a talented organist himself, Kevin knows a good organ when he hears one. In his book *From Paramount to Penistone*, Kevin tells the full story of finding the organ he wanted, then locating a home for it. He calls his search 'How it All Began' and describes his burning ambition as a schoolboy to play the cinema organ; even at a young age he wanted to own one.

In adulthood Kevin's wish to own an organ grew stronger, particularly following his involvement in the installation of a new cinema organ at the City School, Sheffield. He travelled the country looking at organs made by different manufacturers, but none of them produced the sound he wanted. Doesn't this remind you of Glenn Miller's search for the sound he wanted to create?

The life of the Penistone Compton began at the huge Paramount Theatre in Birmingham's New Street on 4 September 1937. At the official opening, organist Al Bollington's performance that day set the style for years to come. Then in 1965 a modernisation programme at the cinema put the organ out of use for fifteen years. Hope springs eternal and there was a short period under its new name – Odeon – when the cinema's audiences were again thrilled by the sound of the Compton, but a conversion of the building into a six-screen cinema complex in the late 1980s signalled the end for the organ there.

Only four Paramount Compton cinema organs were ever built and three were cannibalised over the years to provide spare parts; there was a serious danger that the Birmingham Compton might meet the same end. Fate decreed otherwise: the new owner of the 1,080-seat Regal Cinema at Oswestry, Trevor Harris, bought the Birmingham organ, and it started its new life there on 26 November 1989. Its life at Oswestry was short, though, because the cinema failed to be profitable and was closed in June 1994. It was the advertisement offering the organ for sale that caught Kevin Grunill's attention, with the result that he soon became the new owner of the Compton – but he still needed a new home for it. Initial local interest heralded a good chance that a new home might be found in the Barnsley area, but possible venues were eliminated one by one.

Then, one day, the manager of the then Metro Cinema in Penistone contacted Kevin, who went to see the cinema. While suitable in most respects, the overall height below the stage to house the organ pipes was only 8ft and they required a 16ft clearance. After three years of fruitless searching Kevin reopened discussions with Penistone Town Council. There was clearly enthusiasm on all sides to make things happen; even the problem of the pipe clearance was solved by a plan to cut away the floor.

After many building alterations the space for the Compton was presented to the Penistone Cinema Organ Trust in mid–April 1999 and installation began.

As so often happens, some earlier unrelated event like an act of providence can open up unforeseen possibilities. So it was in 1902 when Penistone Urban District Council made its first move to build a public library. With the help of the Carnegie Foundation a library, council offices and a public hall were completed in 1915; the Town Hall Picture House provided film shows in the public hall, which was also used for Saturday dances.

Penistone's Compton organ. (Penistone Cinema Organ Trust)

The late 1960s brought declining cinema audiences and in 1974 Barnsley Metropolitan Borough Council took over responsibility for the building. A comprehensive refurbishment took place in the 1980s, including the provision of modern fixed seating, which brought Town Hall dances to an end. In 1983, Barnsley MBC decided to close the Metro Cinema; local opposition was strong and responsibility for the cinema was returned to Penistone Town Council.

Thus, in 1994 when Kevin was looking for a new home for the Compton, the Metro was waiting for a new phase of its life to start. What was needed was faith and a brave decision; the rest of the story involves the movement and installation of 7 tons of organ parts in 1999.

Every one of the thousands of parts had to be checked, cleaned and, where necessary, overhauled or replaced, then the delicate and complex work of assembly – with many adjustments to moving parts – began. This labour of love took twelve months and involved many specialist workers and volunteers.

The result is spectacular: the organ, in white and gold, is a feast to the eye. It is fitting that the cinema is now called the Penistone Paramount in recognition of the early days of the Compton organ in Birmingham. The first time the organ was played at Penistone was a day remembered by everyone who attended. Today, regular audiences attend the monthly organ concerts and show their appreciation

Penistone Paramount Cinema.

of the sound of the Compton organ and the commitment of Kevin and his team who have made it possible.

It is not only at the Paramount that theatre organ music can be heard at Penistone; every Thursday at 1 p.m. Kevin plays a programme of popular music at St Andrew's Church. Like the Paramount programmes, the Thursday concerts are very much social affairs, with interval refreshments in the tea room. People come from far and near, share tables and their enjoyment too.

Even before the Second World War there were famous women organists too, including Florence de Jong and Ena Baga. Organ music is enjoyed by ladies every bit as much as the men. They love Ivor Novello's romantic music, but just watch their toes tapping when Kevin plays 'Blaze Away'. The couple behind me said, 'Wasn't that brilliant?' I could only answer, 'The best show in town'.

In September 2006 the old Conn organ at St Andrew's was replaced by an Allen 317EX digital theatre organ, the only model in the UK. Join the queue to hear it!

> For Penistone take junction 37 off the M1 then the A628 towards Manchester
> At Penistone traffic lights turn left towards the town centre
> Turn left on Shrewsbury Road for the Paramount Cinema
> There is a free car park next to the cinema

> Or Penistone Line to Penistone
> Downhill to crossroads, keep left on Shrewsbury Road for the Paramount Cinema

> For St Andrews Church, use the car park in Shrewsbury Road

> Or From Penistone station walk past the Paramount Cinema
> At the town centre turn left into Market Street and High Street
> St Andrew's Church is on the left

Penistone and Well Dressing

Here is a unique Derbyshire tradition found along the Penistone Line! St Mary's Well at Penistone was blessed on Sunday 18 June 2006, the thirteenth time the ceremony was held in the town.

It is a custom that dates back to pagan times and was taken over by the Christian church as a thank-offering for water and its life-giving qualities. There are no written accounts of the earliest days of well dressing, but it is believed that celebrations in our own time arose from a revival of the old tradition at Tissington in Derbyshire – villagers believed their survival from the Black Death in 1348–9 was due to their pure drinking water.

Most of the early well dressing villages were around Bakewell; the limestone on which they stand is very porous and allows rain to soak away almost immediately. So it was that a custom arose of decorating the village wells every year; the day chosen for the blessing was a matter of tradition, sometimes a church festival.

The annual well dressings have now become a beautiful art form, the result of many hours of work by dedicated groups of local people who create large

Penistone well-dressing, 2006.

colourful pictures from flower petals and other foliage including leaves, moss, straw, seeds and fruit. The theme chosen may be religious, but that is by no means a requirement.

The 2006 Penistone celebration began with a procession that formed up by the parish church and followed the White Horse Morris Men and pupils from Spring Vale primary school down to St Mary's Well at Bridge End close to the White Heart Inn. There is believed to have been a well here since 1392 for the use of local people and travellers; a trough by the side of the well still provides water for horses. A short service of blessing with music by the Thurlstone Band, and dancing performed by the Morris Men and schoolchildren, attracted a large crowd and a refreshment stand did good business afterwards. By then the rain had stopped, umbrellas were put away and well dressing photography began.

The Penistone board for the well dressing was filled, according to custom, with wet clay, and their picture 'Feed the World' marked out on the surface, and then the colouring was done with thousands of flower petals.

The left-hand side of the board showed the areas of the world short of clean water and food, while the right-hand side showed our world of comparative plenty. The centre showed how the two areas could come together if those with plenty would help those in want. Below was a representation of the miracle of the loaves and fishes and the feeding of the multitude.

Across the road from the well a special display of small well dressing boards showed the popularity of 'petalling' in schools in the area and at St Andrew's Young Church. The skills the children have already learned are a great encouragement for the future when the present teams of well dressers have retired.

For Penistone take junction 37 of the M1 then follow the A628 west to the junction with A629
At the roundabout turn in to Penistone

Or *By foot follow the Trans Pennine Trail from behind station*
At St John's community centre continue to church across road

Or *Walk downhill from the station past Wentworth Hotel*
Cross the road and go up Church Street to the church

Silkstone Common to Dodworth

Silkstone: The Huskar Pit Disaster Memorial

As so often is the case, a serious accident has to occur before action is taken so that it doesn't happen again. Sometimes tragedy strikes and it becomes clear that it should never have happened in the first place and was a failure to show care and responsibility for others.

It took years and much political pressure – even Royal involvement – before the shameful practice of employing women and children underground in coal mines in the nineteenth century was forbidden. The Mines Act was passed in 1842 ending their exploitation and making illegal the employment of boys aged under 10. Before the Act, many children worked underground at the age of 7; some as young as 5 were employed on simple tasks.

The youngest children seem to have been 'trappers', being required to open ventilation trap doors to let the coal wagons through; others, 'hurriers', hauled the coal wagons to and from the pit shafts. The lightest work was leading horses, where there was room for them, which were used to haul the wagons, or 'corves'. The conditions were appalling, the hours long, and accidents and injuries were frequent.

Perhaps this would have continued for many more years than it did, had it not been for the tragic events of 4 July 1838 at Huskar Pit, Silkstone. That afternoon a thunderstorm broke, accompanied by heavy rain which caused a stream that ran close to the Huskar Pit and its drift access to overflow. Pressure on the doors to the drift built up and when the children inside tried to open them the water threw them back and 26 were drowned immediately. The oldest was aged 17, most of the younger children were aged between 6 and 13, the youngest was only 7. Just six of the children in the pit entrance survived.

Disaster memorial at Silkstone.

Nabs Wood monument, where the children were drowned in July 1838.

The children were buried at All Saints Church at Silkstone in seven graves with the girls at the foot of the boys. One can imagine the effect the tragedy had on Silkstone and the neighbouring villages. An inquest was held at the Red Lion at Silkstone and a verdict of accidental death was reached.

A visit here is really a sad pilgrimage: look for the large monument by the wall close to the corner of the churchyard at Silkstone village crossroads. The names and ages of the children who drowned are listed and the main dedication reads: 'This monument was erected to perpetuate the remembrance of an awful visitation of the Almighty which took place on the 4th day of July 1838. On that eventful day the Lord sent forth His Thunder, Lightning, Hail and Rain . . .'

Perhaps the wording illustrates in some way the thinking of the day. Another monument was erected close to the spot at Nabs Wood, Silkstone Common, where the children died.

> *For Silkstone take junction 37 off the M1 then follow the A628 towards Manchester*
> *On the bypass turn right into the village to the crossroads*
> *Turn left at the church. Kerbside parking*
>
> *For Silkstone Common continue from All Saints Church and cross the bypass*
> *At Silkstone Common, Moorend Lane leads to the wood*
>
> *Or* *Penistone Line to Silkstone Common station. Alight here for both monuments*

Silkstone Common to Dodworth: A Country Walk

Silkstone and Silkstone Common are two villages, separated by the A628 Manchester road. The smaller of the two settlements is Silkstone Common where there was once common grazing land on the hill; the coming of the railway in 1854 and the building of a station there created a separate village.

The Station Inn, the station and the village primary school represent the major buildings in Silkstone Common. There are pubs in Silkstone, also a fine parish church founded in 1000, dedicated to All Saints and known as 'The Minster of the Moors'; the church registers go back to 1549 and there is a notable carved medieval screen.

There was once a horse-drawn railway track that transported coal from early Silkstone Common pits to Silkstone and on to other destinations. As the demand for Yorkshire coal increased dramatically – to provide energy for Lancashire mills and, later, power stations – rail outlets had to be developed. The Woodhead tunnel route via Penistone became vital; to avoid taking increasing numbers of coal trains from the Wath area through Barnsley to reach Dunford Bridge and the tunnel, a more direct track was laid to reach West Silkstone Junction on what is today the Penistone Line.

That railway track now forms the Dove Valley section of the Trans Pennine Trail for walkers, cyclists and horse riders. Firm and level, with regular access

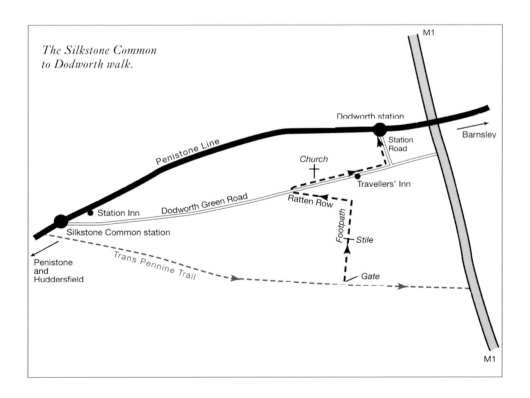

The Silkstone Common to Dodworth walk.

85

points, it offers a magnificent country walk with fine views. By good fortune, the western end of the Dove Valley Trail is very close to Silkstone Common station on the Penistone Line and the Trail then passes Dodworth, which has the next station only a short distance away towards Barnsley. For walkers, another necessary ingredient is refreshment stops: as there are good pubs in both villages, a Silkstone Common to Dodworth walk is highly recommended.

At the bottom of the Silkstone Common station steps turn right, or do the same if leaving the Station Inn. Pass the modern housing development, cross the road and follow the slope of the public footpath down to the former railway track. The old tunnels are blocked westward, so follow the Trans Pennine Trail east until the railway bridge over Moorend Lane is reached. There is access here to the road below and the Huskar Pit tragedy memorial (see p. 83).

Wooden benches have been placed along the track for walkers, but on this bright, cold November morning in 2006 everyone, mainly cyclists, kept moving but not without a greeting. One particular gentleman pushing a wheelchair – a Yorkshire humourist for sure – asked, 'Where have you walked from then?' I thought Silkstone Common was quite ambitious until he said 'We've come from Hull' (well over 50 miles away, of course). I photographed them approaching the famous stone seat here which has a steam locomotive driver carved on one end and a fireman on the other, a reminder of the days of steam. We parted with warm wishes.

Continuing east and close to a plantation are signs of the former Wentworth railway junction which led to Moor End Colliery, a short distance to the south-west.

The next landmark on the walk is a metal field and pedestrian gate on the left and a well-used footpath that leads uphill; beyond a stile and over the brow of the hill, Dodworth church tower is prominent on the left. Downhill now, the footpath leads to a tarmac path towards the church, allotments and a group of buildings (Ratten Row).

The walk to Dodworth: left: the start notice; right: the famous stone seat.

The walk to Dodworth: the footpath landmark and Dodworth Church.

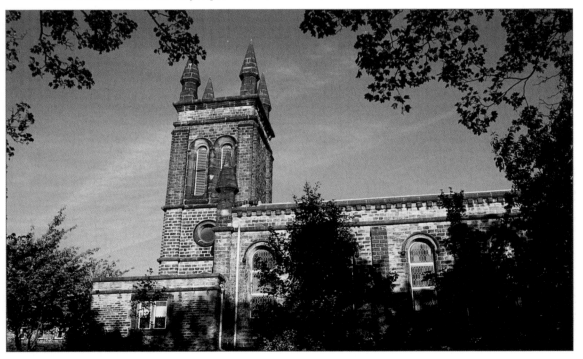

Penistone Line train near Dodworth. (B. Barnsley)

The Traveller's Inn: the end of the journey.

At the corner follow Dodworth Green road to the right past the church; further along at a road junction is the Travellers' Inn (1782), surely once a posting inn.

The pub was something of a find: comfortable, real fires, en-suite accommodation, an excellent menu, immaculate white tablecloths, flowers and pleasant service.

After lunch (if you stop to have some) continue to Dodworth crossroads and turn left at the Co-op into Station Road. Return trains to Silkstone Common are at seven minutes past the hour; allow ten minutes from the Travellers' Inn. Buy tickets on the train.

The time for the walk depends on your walking speed and whether you stop for a rest or to take photographs: estimated time is over an hour, taking account of the footpaths after leaving the Trans Pennine Trail.

Dodworth

Locally the village is known as Dodurth, and 'old time' villagers are called Dodurthers. Barnsley centre is only 3 miles away and junction 37 on the M1 is so close that many people commute daily to Sheffield and Leeds as well as to Barnsley.

Perhaps the one prominent change in Dodworth recently has been the development of its business park. Otherwise the 'muck stack' (spoil heap) from the former colliery is a permanent reminder of Dodworth's nineteenth-century life as a pit village. Life revolved round the pits which were sunk to exploit the rich Silkstone Seam. In those days more than two thirds of local men worked in the pit; women's occupations were mainly domestic service or linen weaving. There was little else.

A tannery existed, giving its name to Tanyard Farm and Tanyard Cottages. Ratten Row is arguable: one suggestion is that the name came from Rattan, the palm stems used in wicker work and from which furniture or baskets were made.

Social life in past generations was focused on the Miners' Welfare Club and the Mechanics' Institute, founded in 1878. It was demolished 100 years later, but while open ensured that village activities flourished, including the Dodworth Colliery Band, the Male Voice Choir, the Nursing Association and the annual flower show.

The parish church of St John the Baptist played an increasing part in village life after the building had been completed; the first service was held in 1846. The traditional Whitsuntide Walks were very much children's events; their procession always ended at Dodworth Hall where they received a bun.

The Dove Valley was a popular place for walking – as it is today on the Trans Pennine Trail. It was called the Dam; as local mines were closed and pumps were put out of use, the constant leakage of water coloured the river and it became known as 'Yellow Waters'. Today things are very different and the Dove Valley has a well-merited reputation for its cleanliness and beauty.

Barnsley

Barnsley's Railway Stations

When a Penistone Line train pulls into Barnsley (now its Interchange station), another in the opposite direction may already be there, or be due any minute. Because of the twin tracks at Barnsley, this is one of the few places where it is possible for Penistone Line trains to pass. The completion of the full interchange facilities currently being built will bring a big improvement for passengers at Barnsley.

In the nineteenth century Barnsley Interchange, formerly known as the Barnsley Exchange station, was inadequate to cope with the several railway

Barnsley Town Hall.

The former Court House station building.

companies wanting to build and operate routes serving south Yorkshire towns through Barnsley, so a second station was opened at the corner of Eldon Street and Regent Street on behalf of the North Midland Railway.

At its opening in 1869 it was known as Regent Street station; the old Court House was incorporated to provide a ticket office and a waiting room and was named Top Station by the locals. It was one of the most handsome station buildings in the whole area, with the Royal Coat of Arms over the main entrance in Regent Street.

In 1873 it opened officially as the Court House station, but by the 1950s, following rail closures and mergers, there was little point in trying to keep two stations open at Barnsley; Court House station was closed in 1960.

Barnsley's regalia.

Barnsley Court House station, 1947. (H.C. Casserley)

Today it is a pub and restaurant owned by the J.D. Wetherspoon group. In the past the building has housed a post office, an auctioneering business, a furniture store and has even been a dance hall.

Barnsley: Locke Park and Joseph Locke

If this large public park had been named after Robert Stephenson or Isambard Kingdom Brunel, visitors would have had no difficulty in making a railway connection, but Joseph Locke? Yet all three were contemporaries and all played a vital role in planning and building Britain's railways in the nineteenth century; they continued the pioneer work begun by George Stephenson and well understood the economic advantages the railways would bring to Britain.

Less has been written about Locke than the others, and when he died suddenly, aged 55, in 1860, there was nothing to show at Barnsley, where he was brought up, to commemorate his life and work. Then in 1861, Locke's widow, Phoebe, bought High Stile Field, presented the 17 acres to Barnsley and donated funds for enclosing the land and laying it out as a public park.

In 1874 Phoebe's sister, Sarah, added 20 acres at the top of the park and built an Observation Tower there (sometimes referred to as a 'Belvedere') in memory of her sister, who died in 1866. Yes – it *does* lean, but it is spectacular, elegant –

and quite safe. A further addition at the lower end of the park, along Keresforth Hall Road, increased the size of the park to about 40 acres.

The car park is at the lower end, with a network of paths leading across and up the hill through a natural wooded area. The trees are mature now, providing many patches of shade that, on a hot day, make the uphill walk especially pleasant.

You cannot fail to see the bandstand as you walk through the trees; every self-respecting park had to have one! It was 1708 before it was completed and proved a very popular asset to the park; even today its high domed roof and its bright colours provide an air of gaiety. Many people, especially the elderly, remember the music and the many 'chance' meetings that were contrived to happen at the bandstand.

The tower remains hidden until the very last moment, as trees cluster round it, but easily seen is the quarry, its gardens and steps a reminder of the quarry and dingle at Shrewsbury. The former fountain is now ablaze with flowers.

The Observation Tower at Locke Park.

The bandstand.

93

The statue to Joseph Locke.

On the higher ground above the so-called ABC steps from the quarry are the four Roman columns that puzzle visitors. They were once on the front of the commercial buildings that stood at the corner of Royal Street. When alterations were made to the façade, they were re-erected in the park, where they make a striking scene.

In pride of place near the top entrance gate is a bronze statue of Joseph Locke by Baron Marochetti, commissioned by the Institute of Civil Engineers and later enclosed by a stone balustrade.

Joseph Locke was born at Attercliffe near Sheffield in 1805 and moved to Barnsley in 1810, where he attended Barnsley Grammar School. When he left school his father, a colliery manager, apprenticed him to George Stephenson, the great railway engineer. Locke worked with him on the Stockton and Darlington and Liverpool and Manchester Railways, acquiring a reputation that led to his being appointed chief engineer on the Grand Junction Railway.

This was more than 82 miles long, connecting Birmingham with the Liverpool and Manchester line. It is held to be the world's first long-distance railway and had many engineering obstacles. Locke set up his main locomotive works at Crewe – this was directly responsible for the vast increase in population there, and Locke even helped to lay out the new town.

His success on the Grand Junction Railway led to his receiving commissions to build railways all over Europe, but many believe he should be remembered particularly for the London and Southampton Railway which he designed to run through embankments and cuttings, thus avoiding the expense of tunnels and permitting high speed running.

Joseph Locke became President of the Institution of Civil Engineers in 1857 and by then knew both Brunel and Robert Stephenson well; Robert had been a close friend of Locke since his early days. All three were heavily engaged in railway building and we owe them a great debt for the railway system we now have, although there have been many route closures.

BARNSLEY'S HERITAGE

THIS PARK
WAS DONATED TO THE TOWN
IN MEMORY OF

JOSEPH LOCKE

RAILWAY ENGINEER
1805-1860
WHO WAS RAISED
IN BARNSLEY

Locke's main lines have survived with one exception, the Sheffield to Manchester route via Penistone and the Woodhead Tunnel. This is very much Penistone Line country; on the Yorkshire side of the tunnel the track is now part of the Trans Pennine Trail, so it deserves special treatment (see Dunford Bridge, p. 99).

For Barnsley Locke Park take junction 37 off the M1 then the A628 towards the town centre
At the first junction turn right on Broadway
Follow the A6133 into Keresforth Hill Road
Look for the church tower ahead and turn right
Locke Street leads into Keresforth Hall Road
Car park for Locke Park is on the left

Or   Penistone Line to Barnsley Interchange
No suitable bus service to Locke Park
Walking distance: over 1 mile

Barnsley: Cawthorne, Cannon Hall, Park and Gardens

For over 200 years Cannon Hall, Cawthorne, was the home of the Spencer family (later the Spencer-Stanhopes), leaders in the area's charcoal iron industry in the late seventeenth century. The date of the house is not known, nor the name of their architect, but we do know that the famous York architect, John Carr, was

Cannon Hall, Cawthorne.

Cannon Hall gardens.

responsible for an extension in 1765. He added two wings, one storey high, to accommodate a dining room and a library and made improvements to the interior, particularly to the pillared entrance hall. In 1804/5 an upper floor was added to the wings; a balustrade extends round the whole of the house, adding to its height and its character. More recent alterations include an oak–panelled ballroom.

The museum has a fine art collection covering the period from the seventeenth to the twentieth century. Included are ceramics, glass, furniture and paintings; of the latter, highly prized is 'Mrs Tuder' by John Constable, one of his comparatively few portraits. Also on view is the Museum of the 13/18 Royal Hussars (Queen Mary's Own) and Light Dragoons.

There are over 70 acres of parkland and beautiful formal gardens, landscaped by the famous garden designer Richard Woods of Chertsey in the 1760s; his work is rare in the north. The walled garden houses the historic pear tree collection and the Muscat vine. Accessible from the garden or the museum are the tea rooms.

The museum is closed in January and February, with the exception of school visits; and open on Sundays only in November, December and March, 12 noon to 4 p.m. The gardens are open all year round (except the walled garden). For detailed opening hours call: 01226 790270.

For visitors interested in family memorials, a visit to All Saints Church, Cawthorne is recommended. The west window has three figures of the virtues in the Pre-Raphaelite style and colour dedicated to Hugh Spencer-Stanhope, and in the north chapel window is a further Stanhope memorial with glass thought to be from the William Morris workshop.

Cannon Hall Farm is located close to Cannon Hall Museum. To reach it, continue past the country park car park, turning right behind Cannon Hall to the farm car park.

Once the home farm of Cannon Hall, supplying food for the household, Cannon Hall Farm today is both a working farm and a popular educational attraction, receiving over 35,000 children annually. Visitors can see a wide range of farm animals and newly born arrivals, with an opportunity for feeding. As well as an indoor picnic area for schools, there are special arrangements to visit the chick hatchery, milking parlour and see a variety of small animals.

The farm is open every day except Christmas Day from 10.30 a.m. to 4 p.m. (October to March) and 10.30 a.m. to 4.30 p.m. (April to September). For details and enquiries call: 01226 790427.

> *For Cawthorne take junction 38 off the MI then the A637 towards Barnsley*
> *Continue to roundabout then right onto the A635*
>
> Or *Penistone Line to Denby Dale or Barnsley*
> *Then bus service 236 (Barnsley–Huddersfield)*
> *Denby Dale White Hart to Cawthorne park gates, or*
> *Barnsley Interchange to Cawthorne park gates*
> *Service runs every 2 hours*

Monk Bretton, near Barnsley: Monk Bretton Priory

The monks who established Monk Bretton Priory in 1154 came from the Priory of St John at Pontefract. Following a disagreement between the two religious houses over the policy to follow for appointing a Prior at Monk Bretton, there arose a dispute that continued until 1281; in that year the Archbishop of York visited the Priory and the monks accepted his authority over them. From that time the house became an independent Benedictine monastery.

Along with other Yorkshire monasteries, Monk Bretton was handed over to the Crown at the Dissolution in 1538 and its valuable assets were dispersed; two pillars and arches of the north aisle of the Priory Church were bought by the then Lord Wentworth and used to build a north aisle at Wentworth Church.

The Priory's land and buildings were bought in 1589 by George Talbot, 6th Earl of Shrewsbury, last husband of Bess of Hardwick; and the Prior's house was converted into a residence. Having passed through the hands of a number of lay owners, the site today is in the care of English Heritage.

The gatehouse is the most prominent part of the now ruined Priory. Although its likely date is early fifteenth century, it appears to have been an expansion of a smaller and older gatehouse on which the later one was built.

Immediately beyond the gatehouse are the remains of the Priory church, outlined by its ruined walls. It was enlarged over the centuries and there is a good view from the site of the high altar through to the west end of the nave. Graves found in the Presbytery are thought to include that of the founder, Alan Fitzswane (or Fitzwain).

As was usual, chapels were built along the transepts (the arms of the crossing) facing east, and on the south side of the nave are doorways used by processions going to and from the cloisters. Although the bases of the cloister walls are intact, nothing remains of the arches and arcades round it. In the cloister wall is a book cupboard.

Domestic buildings such as the refectory and kitchen are south of the cloister. As usual there was provision for running water: a drain, still in good condition, diverted water from the River Dearne and ran beneath the kitchen. The stream also provided a supply for sanitation.

The Prior's house was a substantial and separate building. Prior's Hall, on the first floor, seems to have been almost palatial judging by its size and the quality of its stone work; visitors of importance would have been received by the Prior here. The Prior's private chamber was also impressive; its east wall has a handsome pillared fireplace with a stone hood.

Visitors to Monk Bretton Priory often ask about the ancient stone building that stands to the left as they pass through the gatehouse. Although in the past it seems to have acquired the title of Guest House, it is now thought likely to have been an administrative building.

Monk Bretton Priory gatehouse.

Monk Bretton Priory refectory from the south.

For Monk Bretton Priory take junction 37 off the M1 then follow the A628
towards Barnsley
Turn right on to the A6133
Continue to Stairfoot roundabout then turn left on to the A633
At the next roundabout follow the brown signs to the Priory
Turn right, the gatehouse is straight ahead

Or   *Penistone Line to Barnsley Interchange*
Bus services 31 or 57
Services run every 10 minutes. Journey time: 10 minutes

Barnsley: Dunford Bridge and its Railway Story

Standing in the large car park, a departure point for walks along the Trans
Pennine Trail, the Upper Don Trail sign tells you where you are and a second
sign reads 'Welcome to Dunford Bridge'. But perhaps there should be another
sign that reads 'The station that never was'!

Dunford Bridge former station site.

Looking eastward from here, the Upper Don Trail rises and heads out of sight on its 6-mile route to Penistone. West, towards the road bridge, was the former busy station, its platforms, sidings and turntable have all gone; further west still from the road bridge, the Woodhead Tunnel portals can be seen, the by-road to the village passing close by.

The story of the construction of the line and the tunnel is a fascinating one, as the logic behind it made sense at the time – and for years afterwards. A direct rail connection between Sheffield, the South Yorkshire coalfield and Manchester with hungry power stations and mills on the Lancashire side of the Pennines was clearly a strong motivation to coal owners and railway builders alike.

Joseph Locke (see p. 94) and Charles Vignoles were approached in 1835 to report on the possibility of that connection; Vignoles plan was accepted and he was appointed engineer, but little capital was invested and progress was negligible. He invested in shares himself and eventually work began in 1838; nobody, least of all Vignoles, seems to have realised how difficult the project would be, especially in cutting the Woodhead Tunnel, and he soon found himself in financial trouble and resigned.

In May 1839 Joseph Locke took over the construction of the 42-mile line; his greatest challenge was the tunnel. Like the Ribblehead viaduct in North

Yorkshire, it required an army of labourers to work miles from anywhere. In severe conditions, they needed to be accommodated, supplied and fed; much has been written on their suffering through accidents and illness. Many died.

Only a single bore tunnel was possible because of a cash shortage, but even so it was the end of December 1845 – ten years after the plans had been approved – before a train actually ran from Sheffield to Manchester through the tunnel. It was not long before it became obvious that another track would be needed and everyone had to face the grim prospect of more winter weather while a second bore was made through the Pennines. But it was done: long trains loaded with coal then began to pass regularly from the railway marshalling yards, such as Wath through Penistone, on to Dunford Bridge and through the tunnel.

Woodhead was one of the world's longest railway tunnels in 1845 (3 miles and 13 yards) and the smoke and steam endured while going through must have been dreadful for those aboard passenger trains. Imagine the effect on train crews in open cabs!

When it was decided to electrify the route, a new double track tunnel was bored through and trains from Wath carrying coal began to pass along the new tunnel in 1983 on their way to Fiddlers Ferry power station. It was Britain's first fully electrified railway, known as the Manchester–Sheffield–Wath electrification, but its system (1.5kV DC) became outmoded; it would have been very costly

Woodhead Tunnel portal.

Service track to Woodhead Tunnel.

to replace the power supply, passenger numbers began falling and collieries were closing.

In other words, it was vulnerable and was closed by Dr Beeching: to passengers in 1969 and to freight in 1983. Penistone's importance as a junction for Manchester, Sheffield and Huddersfield disappeared and Dunford Bridge as a station vanished altogether.

The story might have ended there, but for a refusal by the Ministry of Power to allow the National Grid to be routed by means of pylons and overhead high tension cables through the Peak District. Instead, the second Woodhead bore was cleaned of soot and the electricity cables were taken through the old railway tunnel.

A 2ft gauge rail track was laid to carry workers and material to install and maintain the system; this passes below the road bridge from the old station site into the former rail tunnel. Today it looks pitiful in comparison with the original tracks, traffic and tunnels that 'the Woodhead' once represented; better to remember the achievement of Joseph Locke and his army of workers. In those days anything was possible.

> For Dunford Bridge take junction 37 off the M1 then take the A628 west, and continue beyond Penistone
> At Millstone Green fork right on to the B6106
> Cross the A616, then left for Dunford Bridge
>
> Or From Huddersfield take the A616/A6024 to Holmfirth
> Then follow the B6106 Dunford Road
> Fork right through Hade Edge
> Pass Winscar Reservoir to Dunford Bridge
>
> Or Penistone Line to Penistone then Trans Pennine Trail
> (A 6 mile walk – only for the stout-hearted)
>
> Or Bus service 20 from Penistone Market Place
> Infrequent service. Journey time: 30 minutes
>
> Advice: The pub at Dunford Bridge has closed. Instead try the Bay Horse at Hade Edge crossroads, where the meat and potato pie is outstanding.

Stainborough, near Barnsley: Wentworth Castle

Wentworth Castle takes its name from Thomas Wentworth who bought the estate from the Cutler family in 1708. At that time the house was called Stainborough Hall and was built in the Classical style; it was incorporated as the north range of the great house built here later by the Wentworths. Thomas took the title Lord Raby on the death of the Earl of Strafford in 1695, but the bulk of the Strafford estate was inherited by a cousin, Thomas Watson-Wentworth at Wentworth Woodhouse.

Thomas (Lord Raby) was determined to show at Stainborough that his branch of the family was in no way inferior to the one at Wentworth Woodhouse and set about building a house that outshone his cousin's. Through his position as British ambassador in Berlin he secured the services of Johannes von Bodt, the city architect, to design a new east-facing range of the house in the Baroque style. This was fifteen bays wide and was completed by 1713.

Work inside continued until about 1730, including a massive 180ft-long Long Gallery with Corinthian columns at either end. Elaborate carvings and decoration were added throughout and are especially prominent outside, above the three large central windows of the first floor.

Lord Raby's success as a diplomat was rewarded by his earldom as the Earl of Strafford of the second creation, after which he had even greater ideas for his country estate. This he developed in the custom of the day, even to the building of a folly, a mock castle on the top of a hill, the sort beloved of poets and novelists including Sir Walter Scott. Much of it has now crumbled away, but two ivy-clad towers belonging to the gatehouse remain – a romantic monument to medieval days. On completion the name of the house was changed to Wentworth Castle.

Stainborough 'mock' castle gatehouse.

By the time of the 2nd Earl of Strafford, building fashions had changed; he added another new range to the house, this time in the Classical style of Palladio with a six-columned portico and central pediment, a great contrast to the Baroque style of 1713.

At Wentworth Woodhouse there was a similar pattern of events: Thomas Watson-Wentworth was ennobled time and again for his political work, eventually being made Marquis of Rockingham by King George II. He also found his new Baroque mansion had become unfashionable and began to re-build in the

Wentworth Castle: the Palladian wing.

Palladian style. The new house was to have the longest front – 606ft – of any country house in England.

Back at Wentworth Castle, the new building range was less palatial than Wentworth Woodhouse, but in excellent taste. Similar in size to the Baroque wing, all its elements were restrained and harmonious. Much of the architectural design was in the hands of Charles Ross, whose ground floor had five arched windows in the centre and similar Venetian windows at each end of the first floor. In the centre, six huge Corinthian columns supported the pediment containing the crest of a griffin carved by John Platt of Rotherham.

The gardens were reorganised to introduce informal parkland with temples, statues and obelisks. Later generations made significant contributions to the gardens with planted areas and walkways.

Wentworth Castle has special spring opening arrangements during the azalea and rhododendron season. There are over 500 species and garden varieties of rhododendron, including the National Collection of the Falconeri series. These were introduced comparatively recently and their ever-changing colours make the walk up to Stainborough Castle spectacular.

Wentworth Castle ceased to be a family home in 1948 when the house and 60 acres of parkland were sold for educational purposes. Much restoration work was

Wentworth Castle gardens

needed before a teacher training college was opened, but its small size was felt to be uneconomic and it was closed in the 1970s. However, after its facilities were upgraded in 1978, it re-opened as the Northern College of Residential Adult Education.

> *For Stainborough take junction 37 off the M1 then the A628 towards Barnsley*
> *Turn right at the first major turn*
> *At the T-junction take the B6099 and cross the M1*
> *Turn immediately left*
> *At the crossroads see signs for Northern College*

> Or   *Take junction 37 off the M1, then take the A628 towards Penistone*
> *At Dodworth turn left and left again*
> *At the bridge over the M1 turn right for Northern College*

> Or   *Penistone Line train to Barnsley Interchange*
> *Then bus services 23 or 24 to Stainborough College*
> *Service runs every 30 minutes. Journey time: 15 minutes*

Thurgoland, near Barnsley: Wortley Top Forge

For anyone visiting Magna Science Adventure Centre at Templeborough where the wonder of modern steelmaking can be experienced, Wortley Top Forge is an historic predecessor and survivor of eighteenth-century iron making even before steam power, when water had to be harnessed to provide energy.

It was part of Wortley Ironworks (Low Forge fell into ruin) which used the River Don to power its waterwheels; Sir Francis Wortley set up his forge by the river well before 1625. All the raw materials he needed were close by and mills became established in the Don valley using products from Top Forge to make wire and nails.

The date 1713 was important at Top Forge; a date stone near the entrance with the initials MW (Matthew Wilson, manager in 1713) is a reminder of extensions and alterations to the buildings. During the following century a process for manufacturing wrought iron from the brittle and less useful cast iron was introduced. By this time railways were spreading all over the country and Top Forge became famous for railway axles and for bar iron that could be used in many branches of metal manufacturing.

At Top Forge, a guided tour (Sundays only) begins in the cottages where workers lived on the site; much more imposing is Huthwaite Grange, or the 'Gaffer's House', which still stands on the opposite side of the road to Top Forge.

Wortley Top Forge, Thurgoland.

To the left of the forge entrance lane is the Small Dam, which collected water from the River Don that looped all round the site. At one time there was a large dam because of the supplies of water needed to power the two waterwheels for wrought iron production and for the Blower Wheel whose task it was to drive the bellows for the air blast that raised the temperature of the furnaces.

One of the exhibits at Top Forge is a 'faggott': a bundle of sixteen iron bars clamped together which would have been raised to white heat in the furnace. Taken under the massive hammers by crane from the furnace, the bars were welded together and given the shapes required.

It was vital to keep the speed of the waterwheel constant, since the cam wheel that lifted the hammer was linked directly to the waterwheel; as the cam wheel revolved its four or five lobes raised the hammer in turn, which then fell under its own weight. Blows of three tons were possible from this, four or five per minute if the water-wheel revolved once every sixty seconds.

The noise must have been eardrum-shattering and the rain of hot metal flakes during forging required the forge men to wear face masks and thick leather coverings from neck to

Waterwheel and hammer.

Detail of waterwheel.

foot. There was a danger, too, of the work pieces falling as they were being moved by the cranes into, then out of the furnaces to the hammers for forging.

At the rear of the forge is a separate building that housed ancillary services that would have been necessary for repairs to the main machinery. The building also included a foundry and joinery for special orders received by the forge. A machine shop has been installed here, mainly using recent drills, lathes and milling machines.

Top Forge is in the care of Sheffield Trades Historical Society which bought and restored it, thanks to the work of volunteer members. The society maintain it and provide guided tours; Top Forge is only open on Sundays.

> For Wortley Top Forge take junction 35 off the M1 then the A629 towards Huddersfield
> At Thurgoland turn left at the traffic lights (Cote Lane)
> Follow the road downhill and over the bridge. Top Forge is on the left
>
> Or   Penistone Line to Penistone, then bus service 24 from Market Place
> Service runs every 2 hours. Journey time: 15 minutes
>
> Or   Trans Pennine Trail: Access from Upper Don Trail off Cote Lane near the bridge over the river

Overton: Caphouse – National Coal Mining Museum for England

Landmarks that once told travellers of the area's coal mining history have gone forever. The spoil tips have been grassed over, the head gear and winding engine houses of the collieries demolished. Even the piles of coal once delivered outside houses in the pit village and then shovelled into cellars are absent.

Caphouse colliery entrance.

Energy is said to be 'clean' now and our coal needs are being met by imports. Industry no longer uses vast quantities of coal – many railways built to move it have closed down, like branches of the Penistone Line. It has meant the loss of an industry and a way of life for many communities.

Fortunately, the National Coal Mining Museum for England was established to remember the way coal was mined and the impact the industry had on mining communities; over a million people in this country were once employed in coal mining. Caphouse Colliery where the museum is based was a working pit until 1985; in 1988 the Yorkshire Mining Museum was opened here and became the National Museum in 1995. And it is within reach of the Penistone Line!

Because coal seams are close to the surface on the west of this part of Yorkshire, commercial mining began early; the first shafts were sunk at Caphouse in the 1780s. Output justified the building of a colliery railway to take coal to the nearby canal and rail line; the outline of a former spoil tip is still visible close to the Reindeer Inn. The pub's buildings were once called Cap House, hence the name of the colliery.

This is not just a museum with galleries (although these are excellent), but Caphouse has been preserved and restored as if a working colliery; also, all the facilities including a tour underground are *free*. At reception you will be asked if you wish to go underground (this requires a special ticket) and if you wish to do so you will be told when the next tour is available; the underground tour takes over an hour.

The underground tour (look for the yellow arrows on the ground leading to the departure point, the lamp room) is conducted by a guide who was once a miner. The normal security procedure is followed: each person going down receives a

Caphouse colliery: the underground tour at Overton. (National Coal Mining Museum)

National Coal Mining Museum screening plant.

brass check so that numbers coming back ensure that nobody is left behind. Everyone is also issued with a helmet, lamp and battery pack.

This shaft is only modestly deep: 439ft, having been sunk at the end of the eighteenth century. Once down there it is much easier to see how women, children and ponies were employed and how methods and conditions have changed. In particular, safety regulations can be explained, such as use of the miners' Davey lamp. Until the lights are turned off it is quite impossible to imagine what it must have been like to work a whole shift in the dark.

The gallery area nearest reception illustrates how mining families lived (often in poverty) and the changes that have taken place, such as the provision of pithead baths and welfare regulations. There is a fine display of miners' lamps and colliery banners; a colourful community life in mining areas is shown by the strong support for brass bands and sporting competitions.

There is much more to be seen outside: the Coal Interface Galleries concentrate on the problems and dangers of working underground, with special emphasis on traditional methods of cutting coal and the impact of ventilation and mechanisation.

The largest working building at Caphouse is the screening plant; at one time stone was sorted from the coal brought out of the workings on a 'picking belt', but was later screened and washed mechanically before being loaded to be carried away.

Direction signs make it easy to find the engine house. The original steam winding engine was installed in 1876. In this area were the wages office and the pit head baths which were part of the welfare development at the colliery. There is a nice warning notice to the miners at the baths office: 'No money, then no soap, don't ask'. Before the pit head baths it must have been have been a dirty and uncomfortable end to a dark and dangerous working day.

Allow time to visit the stables; the ponies are in retirement now, of course. The custom was to use them to haul tubs of coal from the working face to the pit shaft; a hundred years ago about 70,000 were employed in this way and with one exception (the Shire horse) all of the ponies here spent some time underground.

Beyond the stables are the picnic areas and the fascinating Drift mouth which allowed access to a 'surface drift'. Coal from near the surface was transported mechanically up a long surface conveyor to the screening plant. When workings of neighbouring shafts became linked with Caphouse, the Drift mouth provided ventilation for them.

After the underground experience and the outdoor walking it is a blessing that there is a superb cafeteria near reception and the shop. After all, there is still the restored Hope Pit still to see and the nature trail.

> For Overton, Caphouse take junction 38 off the MI then take the A637 towards Huddersfield
> At the second roundabout (Grangemoor) take the A642 east
> After 2 miles the Caphouse is on the left. There is a car park

> Or Penistone Line: Huddersfield, then bus service 232 (Wakefield service). Stand G
> Service runs at 10 minutes to the hour
> Journey time: 40 minutes
> Bus stop at the Raindeer Inn, close to the museum

West Bretton: Yorkshire Sculpture Park

Yorkshire's heritage of great country houses and estates such as Castle Howard and Harewood House are deservedly well known. In Penistone Line country there are fine examples too, such as that at West Bretton.

A Norman family called de Bretton settled on land here after the Conquest; through marriage and inheritance the estates passed to the Dronfield family, followed by the Wentworths and the Beaumonts. In the seventeenth century Bretton Hall was a substantial timber-built house; this was replaced by a grand house in the Palladian style built by Sir William Wentworth after his marriage in 1720 to the wealthy Diana Blackett from Northumberland. Nineteenth-century additions almost doubled the size of Bretton Hall and there were landscape improvements to the estate.

Today, about 500 acres of this eighteenth-century parkland is open to visitors; 260 acres of which include the Bretton Lakes Nature Reserve, the Bretton Country Park and the internationally renowned Yorkshire Sculpture Park. Bretton Hall is now part of the University of Leeds; its campus is rightly described as one of the most beautiful in Britain.

Yorkshire Sculpture Park. Above: 'Two Forms' by Henry Moore; below: 'The Family of Man' by Barbara Hepworth.

Deer Shelter at Yorkshire Sculpture Park. (Skyspace)

The Yorkshire Sculpture Park is an international open-air gallery for modern and contemporary sculpture set in a beautiful landscape. There are usually at least forty sculptures to be seen on the huge estate and a special gallery exhibition area. Of particular interest outdoors are numerous striking works by Henry Moore and Barbara Hepworth.

In 2006 the eighteenth-century Deer Shelter just below the YSP centre and car park was transformed into a Skyspace, one of a number built by the visionary American artist James Turrell. The project was funded by the Art Fund, Britain's largest independent art charity.

Within the lighted inner chamber of the shelter, seating round the walls allows visitors to study the sky through an aperture in the ceiling. The experience seems to bring the sky into the shelter and even to change its colour. Time is of the essence: perception of the sky from the Skyspace is a gradual and personal thing. On leaving the building the 'outside' sky often seems to be quite different from that experienced inside.

The Skyspace project and the Awareness of Light idea has created an enormous amount of interest. Queuing for access has had to be introduced at busy times.

As well as the gallery in the centre, there is a shop, restaurant and coffee bar, conference accommodation and all the usual visitor facilities. To make the park as accessible as possible, there are ramps for wheelchairs and prams, and scooters are available free of charge for visitors with limited mobility.

In addition to the year-round outdoor sculpture exhibition there are study days and sculpture courses which offer opportunities to work with artists on the workshop site. On bank holidays there are activities for the general public to join and enjoy. Apart from a break at Christmas, the park is open throughout the year.

The Sculpture Park is an independent charitable trust supported by donations and legacies, together with funding from Arts Council England, Wakefield Metropolitan District Council, the Henry Moore Foundation and West Yorkshire Grants (a joint committee of Bradford, Calderdale, Kirklees, Leeds and Wakefield Councils). Recent capital developments have been part-funded by European Regional Development Fund and Yorkshire Forward (the Regional Development Agency charged with improving the Yorkshire and Humber economy).

For West Bretton take junction 38 off the M1 then follow the A637 towards Huddersfield
After 1 mile brown signs mark the park entrance

Or   Penistone Line to Denby Dale
Then bus service 448
Hourly service. Journey time: 30 minutes

Old Moor: RSPB

If you have visited the Royal Society for the Protection of Birds (RSPB) at Blacktoft Sands near Goole or at Fairburn Ings near Castleford but have not been to Old Moor, then you must do so. It is the only Wetland Nature Reserve accessible from the Penistone Line and the Trans Pennine Trail runs right past the site of Old Moor.

Old Moor RSPB wader scrape.

Old Moor sees itself as 'a different kind of nature reserve' but has all the hallmarks of the RSPB; a warm welcome for both birds and people.

The name 'moor' derives from 'morass', which means an ancient wetland. As part of the floodplain for the River Dearne, the land flooded regularly and would have been swampy and marshy; over the centuries the area was gradually drained and converted to agriculture.

From the 1940s onwards much of the site was used as a coal stocking ground for the surrounding mines and was part of the largest coal marshalling yard in Europe. In the 1950s there were 30 mines in the Dearne Valley, employing around 30,000 people. However a small piece of land called Wath Ings, now part of Old Moor, survived as a habitat for birds and wildlife. This haven was fiercely protected from harm by local birdwatchers and in the 1970s it was given special protection by the Yorkshire Wildlife Trust.

After the closure of the mines, the land became derelict, then in 1991 the Barnsley and Rotherham master plan to regenerate Dearne Valley was created. Between 1991 and 1993 £4m was spent by Barnsley Council to create Old Moor Wetland Centre, as it was then known. Several organisations assisted in its creation, including the Wildfowl and Wetland Trust and the RSPB. The council managed the site at first before transferring management to the RSPB in April 2003. The new visitor facilities opened in summer 2004, thanks to funding from the Heritage Lottery Fund, Yorkshire Forward and WREN, among others.

The subsidence that is all too familiar to those who live and work in mining areas created hollows that eventually filled with water and attracted wildlife. The

Pond with coot and its young, at Old Moor.

removal of soil in landscaping former waste tips also helped to transform the terrain at Old Moor into an environment where wildlife would thrive. But it needed a kind hand to manage it and, led by the experience of the RSPB, there are now over 100 hectares of wetlands at Old Moor. Special habitats have been created and maintained to provide ideal conditions for birds and other wildlife. Fens, reed beds, marshland and open water are home to a wide variety of wildfowl and waders, and the ditches are a haven for water voles.

My first visit was a summer one and there were coot with young on the water quietly going about their business. The grasses along the pathways were full of life,

Banded Demoiselle at RSPB Old Moor. (Mike Richardson for RSPB)

attracted by the wildflowers: my favourite small blue butterflies were fluttering about on their journeys. Passing them like jet aircraft one after another were dragonflies of all colours.

Every season has its own identity and activity: the returning migrants in the spring, veracious feeding in the autumn when Fieldfares and Redwings attack the berries while at their most colourful. Then there is the winter feeding by flocks of Golden Plovers and Lapwings.

The tree sparrow project at Old Moor was started in 1994 by a volunteer who has since become an employee of the RSPB. It all began with the installation of nest boxes and the ringing of birds. At that time there were only four recorded pairs of tree sparrows on the site, a reflection of the general decline of the species by over 90 per cent in the past 25 years.

There are now 120 nest boxes around the reserve; combinations of different coloured rings are used to identify individual birds, thus allowing staff to calculate information such as life span, seasonal movements and feeding patterns.

The number of breeding pairs has now risen to 43 and approximately 300 individuals will spend the winter at Old Moor. This is due to the programme of winter feeding on the reserve; the special crop used also benefits species such as yellowhammers, reed buntings and grey partridges. While the population growth of tree sparrows at Old Moor is slowing, numbers in the wider Dearne Valley are rising steadily. As a result of the ringing system it is possible to tell that birds from Old Moor are dispersing up to 15km away.

The main walk along by the Mere and the Wader Scrape, with bird hides on the way, is easy going: visitors with disabilities can borrow a motorised scooter. Bird watching is, of course, a very serious occupation: note the number of binoculars you see in an hour, or indeed the number of tripods hoisted on to shoulders with mounted equipment to capture any view or any bird of importance. The silent tension in a crowded hide and the sense of 'time does not matter' marks the passion of the committed birdwatcher.

Tree sparrow at RSPB Old Moor. (Mike Richardson for RSPB)

Near the visitor centre is a relaxed stroll round the ponds, an intimate view of Old Moor life where water lilies as well as coot and their young delight visitors.

As well as regular events such as sessions of bird watching for beginners and guided bird walks, Old Moor offers exploration and activity days for children and families, especially during school holidays. Bookings can be made for conferences in the Farmhouse Meeting Rooms and there is a well-stocked shop, above which is Gannets Café with a veranda for outside dining and offering a magnificent view over Old Moor. The chicken and mushroom pie deserves to win an award.

> *For Old Moor take junction 36 off the M1 then the A6195 (Dearne Valley Parkway)*
> *At the A633 junction turn right on to Manvers Way*
> *Old Moor car park is on the left*

> *Or   Penistone Line to Wombwell station*
> *Then bus service 60 (Wath on Dearne). Ask for the Pontefract Road/Manvers Way stop*
> *Hourly Service*

Elsecar

Elsecar Heritage Centre

Little changed in the Elsecar area before 1750 when farm work was the main occupation, but in the 65 years that followed the local way of life was transformed. By 1815 Elsecar must have looked and sounded like Coalbrookdale on the Severn in Shropshire; a painting by Philip James de Loutherbourg that he called 'Coalbrookdale by night' shows the reflected flames of blast furnaces and a pall of smoke. Imagination tells us of the noise and the fumes that would have been suffered in the area as well.

Coal had been mined in a very small way in the rural area of Elsecar for many years; after all, the Barnsley coal seam outcropped in the valley and was easily mined, as it was in Coalbrookdale. But without a convenient means of transporting it to more distant markets the mining industry would not have developed as it did.

A plan to open an ironworks locally and an extension of the Dearne & Dove Canal to Elsecar in 1798 provided the spur for growth. The two industries were dependent on each other as they were elsewhere; as in Shropshire, Elsecar saw the establishment of a Coal Tar Works.

The growth of Elsecar into an industrial community will have needed a good deal of capital investment; this was forthcoming from the Earls Fitzwilliam and the Wentworth Estate. Deeper mineshafts needed more efficient winding, also better ventilation and pumping, which stimulated new ideas such as the Newcomen pumping engine and steam winding. The Elsecar New Colliery had opened in 1795 and by 1856 there were seven collieries in and around Elsecar. In addition to this, the Earls did a great deal for their workers and their housing was better than elsewhere; pensions were offered and financial help was available for miners injured at work.

Elsecar's heritage site is today a small but valuable relic of the transformation that took place here in the early years of the nineteenth century. All the local industrial activity and the mechanical

Fitzwilliam Lodge, built as a lodging house for single miners.

*Power House
Square at Elsecar
Heritage Centre.*

systems that supported it needed a repair and maintenance service on a large scale. By 1850 it was clear that the small scattered workshops available could no longer do what was needed.

In 1850 the 5th Earl Fitzwilliam decided to centralise the workshop system and to build what was, effectively, an engineering works at Elsecar. Together with stores, the workshops flourished until the mining industry began to decline; by the 1980s there was little work for the Elsecar engineering works to do and Barnsley Metropolitan Borough Council bought the workshops.

Since the buildings involved were of special architectural and historical interest there has been an ongoing conservation programme and development of the site, now known as the Elsecar Heritage Centre. Regular events and activities are held, including a weekend passenger service on the Elsecar Heritage Railway.

The Heritage Centre is located at the junction of Fitzwilliam Street and Wath Road, with the Market pub on the opposite corner. Today the various buildings are used for very different purposes from when it was an engineering works; the public entrance (free) from the car park on the main street takes visitors under an arch past a clock into what is now Power House Square.

Immediately facing are two large buildings by the chimney; the larger was a machine shop where steam engines were repaired. It is now 'Playmania' children's activity centre. The smaller building was once a saw mill with a saddlery on the upper floor; they are now offices and Hot Metal Press Printers.

Close to the entrance arch is Brambles Tea Room with tables and umbrellas outside; in the buildings on the left are craft galleries occupying what were joinery and paint shops, blacksmiths and offices. At the far end is the former Fitzwilliam station, a private railway station for Earl Fitzwilliam, his friends and important visitors to Wentworth Woodhouse. The range of buildings to the right of the entrance formerly housed a plating shop, a pattern store and a drawing office; today there are furniture makers and interior designers.

Earl Fitzwilliam's private railway station.

Newcomen beam engine.

At the far, or railway end of what is called Ironworks Row are Forge Lane Cottages which once housed an office and pay room for the iron workers; these are Grade II listed buildings.

Beyond and below the workshops a footpath leads to the Elsecar Heritage Railway which runs between Rockingham station and Hemingfield, occasionally in steam. Plans are being actively discussed that would extend the line to Cortonwood retail park. A timetable and information sheet is published by Elsecar Railway Preservation Group and is available at the Heritage Centre. Cross over the level crossing and turn right for the platform and rolling stock; turn left to find another historical treasure: the Newcomen Beam Engine.

Invented by Thomas Newcomen in the early eighteenth century, this type of pumping engine was designed to extract water from Cornish tin mines. The example at Elsecare was built at Chesterfield in 1795 and is the only survivor in its original working location. In view of its great historic and industrial importance it is listed as an ancient monument.

> For Elsecar take junction 36 off the M1
> At roundabout follow brown Elsecar Heritage signs via Hoyland
>
> Or   Penistone Line to Elsecar (limited service, check timetable)
>   Then walk down hill to the Heritage Centre
>
> Or   Penistone Line to Barnsley Interchange, then bus service 325
>   Service runs every 7/8 minutes. Journey time: 24 minutes
>   Alternatively, bus service 227 runs from Barnsley or Rotherham

Chapeltown

Chapeltown: St Mary's Church, Ecclesfield

The name of the village means 'Church in a field' (in Domesday it was Egglesfield), so it was important in Anglo-Saxon days because of its church. Its parish was enormous, about 50,000 acres, and covered parts of Sheffield including Grenoside and Wincobank, as well as Chapeltown, a place of importance in its own right today.

Even before the first recorded evidence of a church here in 1141, preaching went on as was customary under a preaching cross; there is a shaft of one in the south aisle together with a base. Decoration is simple, suggesting a date in the eleventh century.

The nave's massive round pillars are clearly the oldest part of the present church, probably dating back to 1200, and were incorporated at the time of a

Chapeltown: the nave of St Mary's Church, Ecclesfield.

St Mary's, Ecclesfield.

rebuilding in 1478. No doubt the tower was always prominent, but like the rest of today's church is in the Perpendicular style.

During the early part of the church's history, a small cell of the Benedictines from Normandy was established. The date is uncertain, but we do still have the priory and chapel (of 1300) just north of the church. Access to the garden is close to the west end of the church through a brown wicket gate, but is now privately owned. A quiet, unobtrusive visit is possible; arrangements can be made with the occupier for a group visit to see inside the buildings.

The chancel of the church has some memorable woodwork dating back to 1500, including a rood screen separating the chancel and nave. Within the chancel, to the left and right are pairs of carved stalls with misericords: these are hinged seats which, when lifted, show a ledge on which monks could rest during services that involved standing for long periods. Below the ledges carvers illustrated their work, sometimes humorously. A pair of misericords here are typical: one shows the face of an angel, the other that of the devil.

Older than these is the ancient churchwarden's chest, probably from the thirteenth century and made from of a single tree trunk; there are four different locks requiring all the churchwardens to be present when it was opened. Above the chest is the handsome Sir Richard Scott memorial dated 1640; he lies on his side, head resting on his hand. He was a friend of the Earl of Stafford.

At the west end are colourful examples of hatchments which carry the coats of arms of aristocratic families from the area. Of outstanding quality is the Royal Coat of Arms on the north wall of the nave: this was carved and painted at the Sheffield School of Art and Design, now part of Sheffield Hallam University.

There is little medieval stained glass left in the church; following the destruction during the Reformation all there is to be seen are the fragments brought together in the north-west window.

The 'Gatty corner' close to the pulpit is a special place of importance at Ecclesfield: Dr Alfred Gatty was vicar of the parish from 1839 to 1903 and a well-known writer. His *Life at One Living* and his editing of Joseph Hunter's *History of Hallamshire* are his best-known works.

His wife, Margaret, was the daughter of the Revd A.J. Scott, Nelson's chaplain on board *Victory* at Trafalgar. She was a lady of many talents and was best-known for her children's books and editorship of *Aunt Judy's Magazine*. A marble tablet was put in the church on behalf of more than 1,000 children as a token of gratitude for the books she wrote. She was also an accomplished landscape artist and a marine biologist; her collection of seaweed is in the Sheffield City Museum and she published *British Seaweeds* in 1863.

The Scott memorial.

The Gatty family (ten children, of whom two died young) were talented too, all achieving fame. Particularly well-remembered is the Gatty's second daughter, Juliana Horatia; the latter name came, of course, from her grandfather's connection with Lord Nelson.

Juliana was also a children's writer; her contribution to Aunt Judy's Magazine was enormous. From one of her stories came the inspiration for the name Brownies for young girls who later become Girl Guides. Like her mother she was a talented artist; she married an army officer, Alexander Ewing.

Margaret, the eldest daughter, seems to have assisted her mother in editing, but was also an accomplished watercolour artist. The third daughter, Horatia (known as Dot) also worked with her mother and in particular helped with her seaweed collection. Of the youngest daughter we only know of the help she gave her mother in the home and to her father in the parish.

Two of Alfred Gatty's sons were knighted and took high public offices, and one went into the church. Unsurprisingly, they were all talented in their own ways, such as composing music, writing songs and biographies.

The quality of Juliana's writing was so high that she was compared with Lewis Carroll and it is tempting to compare the Gattys with the Brontës. They were both clergy families and have an enduring place in Yorkshire literature, although the children's stories from Ecclesfield are very different from the heart-wrenching tragedies from Haworth. The remarkable feature of the Gatty family is the range and quality of their talents and the contribution they all made to establish the family's reputation far beyond the village where they lived.

The nineteenth-century west window in the church is dedicated to Margaret Gatty and represents the Sermon on the Mount with, below, illustrations of five parables. On the north wall is the Juliana window, showing the Ascended Lord with angels; one of these in the tracery is in the likeness of Juliana.

To the north is the Benedictine chapel with lancet windows and an undercroft and the Priory. Ecclesfield Hall, dating from 1736, occupies part of the former monastic site.

If you come into conversation with any of the church volunteers you will certainly be told about St Mary's tea room. If not, you will find it on the top floor of the Antiques Gallery just round the corner below the churchyard. The toasted teacakes are a dream.

> For Ecclesfield take junction 35 off the M1. Turn towards Chapeltown
> At the next roundabout continue to Chapeltown station
> Turn left towards Sheffield on the A6135
> After about 1 mile turn right at the junction
> Follow signs for St Mary's Church (about ¼ mile)
> Parking by the church gate
>
> Or   Penistone Line to Chapeltown station
> Walk to Market Place (2 minutes)
> Bus service 76 (Sheffield) to Ecclesfield. Ask for St Mary's Lane
> Service runs every 12 minutes. Journey time: 8 minutes

Ecclesfield Priory and Hall.

Rotherham

Rotherham: Chapel on the Bridge

Just a few steps from the bus station, the Chapel on the Bridge over the River Don is one of only four medieval examples in the country; another being at Wakefield, Yorkshire. Its foundation in 1483 came as the result of a will drawn up by John Bokyng, a master at the grammar school, who left 3s 4d towards building the chapel.

Before the Dissolution, the chapel provided travellers with an opportunity to give thanks for a safe arrival; later it became an almshouse, a prison and an isolation hospital. Restored in 1924, the building has five prominent pinnacles along each side and one at each end of the roof ridge; the walls are topped with substantial battlements and there are two windows. The crypt, once used to house prisoners, still has its cell doors.

After the 1924 restoration the chapel was reconstructed and is sometimes used for religious services. It is open to the public occasionally in the summer. For more information contact the Rotherham Visitor Centre at 40 Bridgegate or call: 01709 835904.

Rotherham's Chapel on the Bridge.

All Saints Church

Dear to the hearts of local people, All Saints is familiarly known as 'the Minster'. Indeed, the guide leaflet in the church is headed 'A Guide to Rotherham Minster, the finest Perpendicular Church in Yorkshire'. Pevsner's view of the church is that it is one of the stateliest in the county.

The church certainly does have a perfect and spectacular position in the centre of the town, its 180ft-spire soaring above All Saints Square with its fountain, seats and brilliantly coloured umbrellas. Surrounded by shops, this ancient building is a successor to Saxon and Norman churches on the site. Building of the present church began in 1409, and like the Chapel on the Bridge, it is crowned by pinnacles and battlements.

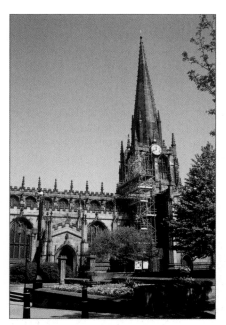

Rotherham: the Minster.

'Monumental' is another of Nikolaus Pevsner's descriptions of the church and this applies both within and without. The huge nave has an oak roof decorated with 77 carved and gilded bosses; the capitals of the pillars have carved foliage. Behind the leaves are examples of Green Men, spirits once venerated in pre-Christian days. One authority gives the number in All Saints as 'over 20', while another claims 'over 30'.

The roof in the chancel is of particular beauty; its roses and bosses were coloured in 1873. Much earlier is the Tudor vaulting below the tower which dates from 1420 and is typical of work done at that time in some of the most famous churches in the land, including St Mary Redcliffe in Bristol.

Do not miss the Jesus Chapel on the south side of the chancel; this was built by Thomas Rotherham (born Thomas Scott in Rotherham) in 1423, who became Lord Chancellor of England and Archbishop of York. He was baptised in the Norman font close by.

> For Rotherham take junction 35 off the M1 then the A629 to the inner-bypass roundabout on the A630 (Sheffield Parkway)
> Take the third exit (Bridge Street), then left for the multi-storey car park at the bus station
>
> Or   Take junction 34 off the M1, then the A6109 to the roundabout, then the A629 as above
>
> Or   Penistone Line to Meadowhall Interchange
> Then bus service X78
> Service runs every 9 minutes. Journey time: 16 minutes

Rotherham: Clifton Park Museum, Clifton Lane

Money from iron-founding paid for the building of Clifton House in 1782–3. Designed by John Carr of York, it had been commissioned by Joshua Walker, whose father, Samuel Walker, was the highly successful iron-founder.

The house was built in the Classical style, with an impressive Venetian window above the pillared portico. The wide pediment occupies much of the façade and emphasises the importance and influence of the family. Much of their wealth came from the casting of cannon for which they had a deserved reputation; many of the cannon used at the Battle of Trafalgar in 1805 – indeed on board HMS *Victory* in particular – came from the Walkers' iron works at Rotherham. At the bicentenary of the Battle of Trafalgar in 2005 and the celebration of the life of Lord Nelson, the contribution of Rotherham and the Walkers was remembered.

Today, Clifton House and its beautiful park belong to the people of Rotherham. The museum's exhibits illustrate the history of the district and help to preserve local heritage. Of special interest to lovers of fine pottery are the Ceramics Galleries on the first floor; the most important collection of Rockingham Porcelain in the country is on display there and its connection with Wentworth Woodhouse is described on p. 132. Fortunately both coal and china clays were available in the Swinton area and by the 1740s pottery for local use was already being produced.

Clifton Park Museum.

Above: Waterloo Kiln.
Left: Rockingham porcelain. (Rotherham Libraries,
Museums and Arts Service)

Although the Swinton Pottery was successful, partners in the firm with interests in the Leeds Pottery as well seemed to have decided to abandon production at Swinton. With financial support from the 2nd Earl Fitzwilliam in 1806, the Brameld family were able to continue the pottery; experiments with clays and glazes led to the production of new wares.

A second financial crisis in 1826 was averted by more support from Earl Fitzwilliam and led to the pottery being given the name Rockingham. The Wentworth family crest of a griffin became the mark of the pottery and it was the development of porcelain for table wares and figures that created the reputation the name enjoys today.

The special, expensive orders placed with the Rockingham works, on which the company depended, were not really economic and poor business conditions in the early eighteenth century meant that closure became inevitable. With no producers willing to take over the business, assets were sold in 1843 to repay the money loaned by the Earl.

It is appropriate that such a fine collection of Rockingham pottery and porcelain should be on display at Clifton House, so close to the original pottery.

The Swinton site of the Rockingham works has just the surviving Waterloo Kiln of 1815 and the Pottery Ponds nearby to be seen. Look for the small car park on the right of Blackamoor Road (the B6092) just west of Swinton, en route to Wentworth. A public footpath leads to the ponds, then behind a private house to the kiln, set among trees.

For Swinton take the A633 from Rotherham
After about 4 miles, at the roundabout take the B6092 on the left
See Rotherham for directions from distant points

Rotherham, Templeborough, Magna Science Adventure Centre

They don't do things by halves in South Yorkshire: exemplified by the M1 Tinsley Viaduct with two sets of carriageways, one above the other, two huge cooling towers beside it on one side, the vast Meadowhall shopping centre on the other and, less than a mile away, Magna, more astonishing than all the rest.

Those unfamiliar with a steel town will be unprepared for the scale on which steelmaking was carried out here. Magna towers over the Sheffield road at Templeborough, occupying so much ground and air space that a major air terminal looks small by comparison. It is only when you watch the steelmaking processes at the Big Melt Show that the size of the operation can be believed.

The secret behind Magna's success with visitors is its interactive experience: from the moment of arrival, light, colour and sound command attention. Young people are offered hands-on experience with electronic equipment and are encouraged to make discoveries and find out answers to questions put to them. For the very young, large screens everywhere show animated adventures.

Pavilions on different levels, accessible by lift or stairs, illustrate the elements of air, fire, water and earth. Experiments with air show how music is created, with water how waves are formed and in the earth pavilion allow a JCB to be controlled to dig out raw material for industry.

But it is steelmaking that made the district famous and created a history of its own. The Fire Pavilion vividly focuses the power of fire; close to it along a high walkway visitors can watch and hear the Big Melt Show. This is where the crowds collect and where many people for the first time learn what steelmaking is all about.

The building's original usage is recreated by the use of every possible visual and sound effect. The thunder of the arc furnace and the Big Melt, the movement of machinery and the commentary from the PA system are mind numbing. Strobe lights flash, cascades of sparks and clouds of steam emerge from the furnace and spotlights on moving gantries overhead direct attention in turn to the different manufacturing processes. The question many ask after seeing the Big Melt for first time is, 'Did men have to spend their working lives like this?'

The use of modern technology today justifies Magna's claim that theirs is a world without limits; where almost anything is possible. New features planned for 2007 include an

129

(Photographs courtesy of the Magna Science Adventure Centre)

exhibition on pioneering torch technology in steel manufacturing and another on science and technology associated with sport and fitness.

Even the great reception area with its never-ending 'shop' displays is overlooked by enormous video screens alive with colour and movement. Books are a minor department here – the visual is everything – well, almost everything; the restaurant and Terrace Café are nearby.

All areas are accessible for visitors with disabilities and wheelchairs are available free of charge from the information desk. Parking is no problem. Apart from the Christmas and New Year holidays Magna is open daily from 10 a.m. to 5 p.m. In winter it is closed on Mondays. For more information call: 01709 720002.

> For Templeborough Magna take junction 34 off the M1 then follow the slip road to the roundabout.
> Continue on lower viaduct then pick up the A6178
> Pass Magna building and follow 'P' signs
>
> Or   Penistone Line to Meadowhall Interchange
> Bus service A1 from stand C4 (destination Rotherham)
> Service runs twice hourly via Magna. Journey time: 9 minutes

Catcliffe, Rotherham: The Glass Cone

Ask anyone to name the industries that made Rotherham and Sheffield famous and there would be no hesitation: iron, steel and cutlery manufacture. Yet at Catcliffe there is compelling evidence of an early and unlikely candidate for inclusion: glass making.

Catcliffe glass cone.

Glass cones were the equivalent of the kilns that were a feature of the Potteries landscape in and around Stoke-on-Trent, but glass cones were hardly to be expected in Rotherham or Sheffield. There are only three survivors in the country as a whole; the Catcliffe example is the earliest and most complete of them all.

The glassworks of which it was part was established by William Penney in 1740; visible traces confirm that there was also a second cone at Catcliffe. Penney had an interest in the Swinton Pottery, later to be known as Rockingham (see p. 128).

Penney's factory at Catcliffe produced a variety of glass including bottle and window glass, and remained in production until 1901. The base of the Catcliffe cone is made from stone, the upper, curved work from brick. The arches at ground level show the arrangement for varying the draught for the furnace.

An information panel placed on the site by Clifton Park Museum at Rotherham adds the curious facts that the cone was used to house prisoners of war in the First World War and was employed as a canteen for workers during the General Strike of 1926. In either case it was an unattractive venue to say the least.

*For Catcliffe Glass Cone take junction 33 off the M1 then the A630
(Sheffield Parkway) towards the Sheffield Centre
Fork left on to the B6533 towards Catcliffe
Turn left at the bottom of slip road towards Catcliffe
Continue under the railway bridge then turn left into St Mary's Drive
After 50 yards turn left into Tristford Close
Catcliffe Glass Cone is on the left behind sheltered housing*

*Or   Penistone Line to Sheffield Interchange
Then bus service 132 from stand C3 (destination Rotherham)
Service runs every 20 minutes. Journey time: 34 minutes*

*Or   From Meadowhall Interchange bus service 261
Infrequent service. Journey time: 20 minutes*

Wentworth, near Rotherham

Wentworth village was in existence long before the arrival of the Wentworth family, who adopted the village name as their own after settling on the land. The exact date is not known, but in about 1300 the Wentworths and the Woodhouses became linked through marriage.

Family influence, and later, power, meant that Wentworth became an 'estate' village, very much in the control of the big house. Many of the villagers were tenants of Wentworth Woodhouse and worked for the families who in turn owned the estate. The age of many of the cottages built for the Wentworths can be guessed from their timber framing, but the hand of the family is shown more clearly by the two churches, both dedicated to the Holy Trinity.

The older of the two, the 'Old Church', was first established as a Chapel of Ease to deal with burials; due to dilapidation it needed restoration in the fifteenth century and again in the seventeenth century. By the 1860s its condition had deteriorated again – so much so that a new church was decided upon by the 6th Earl, who met the cost. All that is left of the Old Church today is the tower, the south wall and the Lady Chapel; monuments to the Wentworths also remain.

The 'New Church' is just over the wall from the old churchyard and is a splendid building designed by the famous architect J.L. Pearson, whose greatest work was Truro Cathedral. Pearson's design was in the Gothic revival style with a particularly beautiful marble floor in the chancel. The spire is nearly 200ft tall and can be seen for many miles.

Church Walk (locally often called Back Lane) is an attractive avenue from the church to Hague Lane bordered in spring with thousands of daffodils. Cross with care here if you wish to visit the Wentworth garden centre, which stands on the site of the eighteenth-century kitchen garden of Wentworth Woodhouse.

Each generation of family at Wentworth Woodhouse has contributed to making the village what it is today; including, for example, the Mechanics Institute, built in about 1822 with library and educational facilities, the Barrow School and the even earlier Wentworth almshouses.

Wentworth had two windmills; one was quite close to the main gates to the park, and both have been successfully converted into homes. Coal mining was a major source of income for the estate, but it was not until after the Second World War that open-cast mining was out of necessity inflicted on the park itself. Mercifully it has gone now and the damage caused has been covered over.

Unusually, the family became connected with pottery and porcelain production that had been based on estate land at Swinton Old Pottery since 1745. When the family-run business ran into financial difficulties in the early 1800s, the Bramelds sought help from Earl Fitzwilliam; with his support they were able to continue production of pottery and porcelain.

Rockingham porcelain, as it became known, was internationally acclaimed and there is a fine collection at Clifton Park Museum at Rotherham (see p. 128).

For travel information see under Wentworth Woodhouse.

Wentworth, Rotherham: Wentworth Woodhouse

When a huge country house like Wentworth Woodhouse has successively been the family home of the Wentworths, Watsons and the Fitzwilliams over the centuries, its authority and responsibility naturally extended far beyond the boundaries of Wentworth Park. Thus it was at Wentworth, where the house and park provided employment for many local people; an ideal estate village, it has also been granted amenities to improve the quality of life of the inhabitants.

As was so often the case in the past, it was a marriage between two landowning families that founded the power which brought with it great aristocratic titles. Here it was a marriage between the Wentworths, whose name came from that of the village, and the Woodhouses.

By 1587 the estate had been inherited by Sir William Wentworth, whose son Thomas became 1st Earl of Strafford in 1640; only fragments of the house he built remain today. Sadly he only had one son, William, the 2nd Earl, who died childless, resulting in the loss of the title; what did survive was much bad feeling in the family regarding their inheritance. The 2nd Earl left the estate to his sister's son, Thomas Watson of Rockingham, an outcome disputed by the sons of the seven brothers of the 1st Earl who asserted that it should have passed down the male line.

When Thomas Wentworth, Lord Raby, one of the claimants, bought an estate at Stainborough and built Wentworth Castle, a house-building rivalry began (see p. 103). He and Thomas Watson, who became Marquis of Rockingham, tried to outbuild each other; ultimately Wentworth Woodhouse became the larger and more palatial. This was the work of the architect Henry Flitcroft, who was

Wentworth Woodhouse and its enormous façade.

succeeded by John Carr of York. Its great front extends 606ft, the longest of any English house. The vast portico carries the Rockingham motto, *Mea Gloria Fides*; 'Fidelity is my Glory'.

Oddly, Wentworth Woodhouse has two 'fronts' (some observers say two houses back to back), the West Front, or Back Front, built first and facing the village of Wentworth, and the East Front facing the park.

Both houses were to become educational establishments: in the case of Wentworth Woodhouse the East Front and stable block were eventually used by the West Riding County Council to house the Lady Mabel College of Physical Education (Lady Mabel was the 7th Earl's sister). It closed in the 1980s and the house is now privately owned and no longer opens to the public.

Much has been written about the interior and there is no shortage of illustrations showing the grandeur of the State rooms. The Grand Staircase by John Carr leads from the Pillared Hall to the Marble Saloon, so-called because of its wonderful marble inlaid floor. The pillars which support the gallery surrounding the room also appear to be of priceless marble, but are in reality a marble substitute called scagliola. This is a plaster applied to the surface of stone columns and made from sand, lime and gypsum (from which plaster of Paris is produced), and crushed stone to give the desired colour, then polished. Many of the craftsmen who specialised in scagliola were Italian. The 60ft-sq. room is decorated with sculptures and statues.

The Needle's Eye, Wentworth Woodhouse.

Beyond the Marble Hall, to the north and south, is a succession of great rooms including the State Dining Room and the van Dyck Room. Of particular interest is the Whistle Jacket Room with its extravagant gilt plasterwork; it took its name from Lord Rockingham's famous racehorse, whose painting by George Stubbs once hung here. The horse is said to have won as much prize money as was spent on building Carr's enormous stable block, which stands alongside the drive from the main gate. Carr's work can also be seen along the façade of the house; his work in the 1780s raised the wings by another storey and added their Classical porticoes.

Carr worked for many years at Wentworth Woodhouse, including designs for the family mausoleum in the park and lodges at the gates.

Great landowners loved decorative features in their parkland such as mock castles and medieval ruins. Wentworth Woodhouse was no exception and had plenty of space for these so-called follies.

Near the main gate to the park is a view of one of the most curious: the Needle's Eye, a

45ft pyramid built in about 1728. Its archway is believed to have been inserted later. Cross Cortworth Lane and walk past the Old Builder's Yard; look up the private road through the trees for a distant view of the Needle's Eye. For a closer inspection, continue towards the road junction and fork left on to Coaley Lane; just beyond a lodge gate on the left is a public footpath leading to the site of the Needle's Eye. The view is splendid.

Also on this side of the park is the quaintly named Hoober Stand. This three-sided tower standing at about 100ft high is a monument to the victory over the Scots at Culloden in 1745. The architect, Flitcroft, was responsible for much of the east front of Wentworth Woodhouse. His choice of a triangular construction seems to result in a changing view of the cupola as one walks round the tower. It can easily be reached by car in the little village of Hoober from which it takes its name.

Even taller than Hoober Stand is Keppel's Column, which stands at 115ft above the modern houses in Thorpe Hesley on the other side of the estate. For the motorist leaving the M1 at junction 35, it commands attention along the road to Rotherham; an attractive view is possible by turning left into Admiral's Crest. The monument was designed by John Carr for the Marquis of Rockingham in support of Admiral Keppel who had been held responsible by the Government for a naval defeat by the French in 1777. He was eventually acquitted of blame and the monument sought to celebrate a political victory as well as restoring Keppel's reputation.

For those visitors wishing to walk to the follies and other places of interest on and around the estate a booklet entitled 'Six Walks around Wentworth' is recommended. It is on sale at the village store.

Hoober Stand.

Keppel's Column.

> *For Wentworth Woodhouse take junction 35 off the M1 then the A629 east*
> *Turn left into Thorpe Hesley. Follow signs to Wentworth*
> *Pass the garden centre and on to the T-junction*
> *Turn right on to Cortworth Lane for park*

> *Or   Penistone Line to Barnsley Interchange*
> *Bus 227 into Wentworth Cortworth Lane. Bus stop outside park gates*
> *Hourly service. Journey time: 37 minutes*

Meadowhall

Meadowhall claims to be one of the most accessible shopping centres in the UK, with over 12,600 free parking spaces and interchange access to and from trains, buses and, of course, the Supertram.

Meadowhall is home to over 270 stores: all the national names are represented while shops in The Lanes sell goods which are a little more unusual. The Meadowhall dome linking the arcades, such as Market Street and High Street, is familiar to the thousands of motorists who rush by on the Tinsley viaduct. The size of the shopping centre prompted the management to provide a shopmobility scheme and special care for the disabled. The free self-drive scooter hire and wheelchair hire, parking spaces, toilets and other facilities have gained Meadowhall a well-deserved award.

A crèche caters for children aged between 2 and 8, and there is an indoor play area 'Little Tikes' for the supervision of young children. It is perhaps not surprising that one of the latest PA announcements on a train arriving at Meadowhall said 'This is Meadowhall. Will all children take their parents with them'. Wonderpark, Meadowhall's amusement arcade, offers everything from ten-pin bowling to the latest videogames.

Needless to say, visiting Meadowhall needs practice; window shopping can be enjoyable but it is nice to find the things you came to see. An information desk

The entrance to the Meadowhall shopping centre.

Above: 'Teemers' sculpture at Meadowhall.
Right: The domed interior.

(with a real officer ready to swing into action) is the first contact visitors have as they arrive at the shopping centre from the Interchange. Maps and directions are available and further information points can be found in each of the shopping arcades on both levels.

A wide selection of coffee shops and restaurants is available, and the stores at Meadowhall stay open 'fashionably late' from October through to Christmas. Perhaps this is an illusion, but getting *into* Meadowhall always seems easier than getting *out*.

If travelling to and from Meadowhall by public transport, allow plenty of time to walk, along with crowds of others, to Supertrams, buses or trains. Platform 4 for the Penistone Line is the furthest platform – and the service runs hourly during the week and every two hours on Sundays.

Meadowhall: Sheffield and its Supertrams

Sheffield's trams have always enjoyed a good reputation – and not only among the city's own citizens. With their low fares, efficient service, familiar and handsome tramcars, the trams were already an institution by 1939.

However, the Second World War brought damage, wartime neglect and deterioration. Even worse, postwar attitudes favoured new forms of transportation; trams were thought 'old hat' – the bus and the car ruled. In 1951 a decision was taken to replace Sheffield's trams with buses and the last of the postwar trams ran in 1960.

So it remained, until urban traffic began to grind to a halt due to congestion. Weaknesses in the bus system led to more people using their cars, and bus lanes designed to help reduce journey times did not tackle the root of the problem. It was the success in Europe of Light Rail systems – in Manchester, too – that pointed the way forward.

This system employs a surface rail along streets and on segregated tracks with powered articulated cars carrying large numbers of passengers. The cars have to operate flexibly, negotiating tight curves and steep inclines; dedicated tracks provide and protect the cars' right of way.

In December 1989 Parliamentary powers were granted for the operation of South Yorkshire Supertram Ltd with project costs of about £240m, much of which, it was announced, would be met by the Government. The official opening took place in 1994. Once again familiar names from the old tram system reappeared: Malin Bridge became a terminus once more, the former Intake route was covered along City Road by the Herdings Supertram, and Attercliffe figured as a stop once more, now on the way to Meadowhall.

It is the Meadowhall route which has caught the public imagination, not only because the terminus is at the immensely popular shopping centre. The Interchange is also served by trains and buses.

The dedicated track has fewer stops than other parts of the Supertram system, but its route crosses and re-crosses existing and former railway lines as well as the Sheffield–Tinsley Canal and the River Don. Prominent on the skyline is the Arena/Don Valley Stadium.

Among improvements made to the design and operating systems of the Supertrams are elevated platforms at stops to allow level access to tram doors, and tactile strips to inform blind people where the doors are for boarding. Apart from concessionary fares for South Yorkshire residents, visitors can make fare savings by buying a Day Rider ticket which allows unlimited use on the day of issue.

As for comfort, gone are the boneshaker days of wooden bench seats: interiors are now pleasing to the eye, and journeys comfortable, quiet and smooth. Each vehicle, which consists of three articulated units, can carry numbers of passengers barely dreamed of before the Supertrams arrived; at the same time, modern design has made possible adequate space for wheelchairs and prams.

Sheffield Supertram.

While a Supertram stop serves Sheffield rail station and is just across the road from the transport Interchange, the first contact many people from outside the city have with the Supertram is at Meadowhall. Although many shoppers continue to arrive by car, the planners who delivered the Supertrams to Sheffield concluded, rightly, that the day would come when many people would prefer to leave the car at home if there was a convenient and comfortable alternative.

Whether you are bound for the Meadowhall shops or the attractions of the city, the Supertram is your best choice.

> *For Sheffield take junction 33 off the M1 then the A630 (Sheffield Parkway) to the city centre*
> *Car park notices in city centre*
>
> Or *Penistone Line to Sheffield*
> *For Meadowhall take junction 34 off the M1 to car park*
>
> Or *Penistone Line to Meadowhall Interchange*

Sheffield

Sheffield: Abbeydale Industrial Hamlet

Few industrial museums have such an educational and social impact as the Industrial Hamlet at Abbeydale. It was a place where employees lived as well as worked; their cottages still stand in a row close to the entrance to the site, which is truly a hamlet rather than just a work place. When the cottage gardens were laid out where the coach park is now, the hamlet must have seemed totally rural.

Because waterpower was essential for Sheffield's growing industry in the seventeenth and eighteenth centuries, mills were established where fast-flowing streams could drive their waterwheels. It was this factor and an abundant supply of industrial raw materials that was responsible for the foundation of metalworking in Sheffield, and in particular for the development of its cutlery industry.

The massive Jessop Tilt Hammer, once used at Jessop's Brightside Works, displayed at the entrance to the Abbeydale Hamlet, creates excitement even before you have bought your entry ticket. It needs a big leap of imagination to believe that waterwheels could provide the power to operate these tilt hammers and to forge a steel blade between two strips of wrought iron. This was the main process in manufacturing agricultural blades such as scythes and grass hooks,

Sheffield: Abbeydale Industrial Hamlet.

The Jessop tilt hammer and hull waterwheel.

although the Abbeydale works was unusual in carrying out all the processes from raw materials to finished products.

An audio system can be used to follow the various stages of scythe production; on entering the open quadrangle of buildings past the gift shop (ticket office) and former workers' cottages, the buildings on the right are ranged visually in a kind of production line.

In the far right-hand corner steel-making processes took place. First, clay pots had to be made and fired; these crucible pots were later charged with basic raw material and lime which acted as a flux when placed in the crucible steel furnace. The melt required was at a temperature of about 1,550°C and took three to four hours; once the contents were molten the liquid was poured into a mould in the Teeming Bay.

The cast steel ingots formed were taken from the moulds and, when cool enough, were tested for quality; after being reduced in size they then went to the Tilt Forge.

Of all the operations at Abbeydale, those at the Tilt Forge were almost beyond belief: the very size and power of the huge spur wheel driven by the waterwheel outside, the girth of the main driving shaft and, most of all, those two great hammers being raised and then falling on to the anvils by their own weight. The heat from the hearths and the noise from the great hammers must have tested the forge master and his assistants to the limits of their endurance.

Forge welding required such high temperatures that a Blowing Engine was necessary to provide the draught for the hearths. It was driven by its own waterwheel, the engine's two great arms forcing pistons up and down to roof level, feeding air through pipes to all the hearths in the forge.

Grinding hull.

Without the water stored in the dam behind the Tilt Forge, the waterwheels would not have been able to keep the operations going and in 1855 a steam engine was put in as a reserve of power if the water level were to fall too low.

The strips of welded metal had yet to be shaped, hardened and tempered before their edges could be ground. The enormous grindstones (about 6ft in diameter) stood in water troughs, for unless the temperature during grinding was controlled, the cutting edge of the blades would be affected. The Grinding Hull had its own large waterwheel.

Finishing required further processes carried out in Hand Forges close by: some scythes had riveted handles and needed holes to be bored for this, some adjustments were made to fit the handles and finally painting had to be done to avoid rusting of the metal.

Allow time for the Manager's House and the cottages. Refreshments and toilets are available on the site.

> *For Sheffield Abbeydale Industrial Hamlet take junction 33 off the M1 then the A630 (Sheffield Parkway) to roundabout, then left A6102 ring road*
> *Continue to the A61, turn right towards Sheffield*
> *Turn left at Abbey Lane lights, B6068*
> *Continue to Abbeydale Road. A621 and turn left*
> *Industrial Hamlet on left, parking on site*

> *Or Penistone Line to Sheffield*
> *Bus service 97 from High Street near T.J. Hughes (stop HS2)*
> *Service runs every 15 minutes. Journey time: 20 minutes*

Sheffield: Beauchief Abbey

Since the abbey's alternative name is the Church of Thomas à Becket, some explanation is needed. The abbey might well never have existed but for the murder of Thomas à Becket in Canterbury Cathedral by knights who believed they were serving King Henry II, who, in fury had shouted 'Will no one rid me of this turbulent priest?'

The crime touched many people deeply: the King himself made a penitential pilgrimage to Canterbury in 1174 and those who could, tried to show their grief in a practical way. One of those was Robert Fitzranulph, who granted land for the building of an abbey at Beauchief.

And what a site it was! Its lonely and beautiful countryside had the advantage of a stream which ran into the River Sheaf, ensuring a dependable water supply as well as a source of fish for food from the usual fishponds. Praemonstratensian canons arrived in 1176 and started building work at Beauchief; further grants of land helped to support them and the growing abbey.

Although Beauchief was not large, it was a busy place; apart from the canons who lived there and the religious activities within the abbey, lay brothers and employees worked on farms and in mines on abbey land. This became extensive as further gifts were made by landowners; all this and care for the poor and sick came to an end in 1537 when the abbey was dissolved on the orders of King Henry VIII.

The abbey lands were sold to Sir Nicholas Strelley of Nottingham; his descendants held the estate for over 100 years until marriage transferred it to the Pegge family. The abbey buildings had long become ruined and the stone was used by the Pegges for building Beauchief Hall in 1671; they also had a little church built on to a surviving tower as a private chapel.

Today, the surroundings of Beauchief are as beautiful as ever, but modern life in the form of Beauchief golf course has taken over much of the landscape. Of the ruined abbey itself, the west tower, once part of the old west wall and smaller than it once was, is the most prominent feature. It has a fine arched and moulded doorway in the Early English style; to the north and south are open arches, both brought from elsewhere on the site, the north arch leading to the abbey grounds.

Within the tower is a spiral stairway leading to the roof, not open to the public as it lacks a parapet; safer is the so-called vestry on the opposite side of the tower, where tea and biscuits are served to visitors on Sundays.

The 1660 church is tiny compared with the nave of the medieval abbey, which excavations have shown was 200ft long; the High Altar was near the wall that divides the abbey grounds from the golf course.

Most of the church contents are contemporary with the building; the first service was held in 1662, so the box pews and the altar are likely to date back to this time. A special high-sided pew for the Lord of the Manor had its own fireplace. Memorials to the two important estate families abound. Outstanding because of its size and quality is the 1844 memorial to Elizabeth Pegge Burnell with two figures depicting Charity and carved by Sir Henry Weekes RA.

*The Chapter House and church altar at
Beauchief Abbey.*

Outside, excavations have shown the existence of a small cloister and refectory, both on the customary south side of the abbey church. A length of tall and ancient wall still stands at the east end of today's church; otherwise one has to imagine the nave, choir and chancel of the abbey. Stones from the Chapter House were uncovered in the twentieth century, showing it to have had two central piers and a polygonal east end; the mound close by which may conceal valuable information has been left untouched because of a burial on top of it.

Beauchief is a popular Sunday afternoon visit (regular services are held in the church); parking is limited along narrow Beauchief Abbey Lane and there is a turning place a short way past the abbey.

> *For Sheffield Beauchief Abbey take junction 33 off the M1, then the A630
> (Sheffield Parkway)*
> *Turn left on to A6102, ring road*
> *At A61 turn right towards Sheffield*
> *At Abbey Lane lights turn left, B6068*
> *Continue past the roundabout*
> *After ¼ miles, at brown sign turn left to abbey*

> *Or   Penistone Line to Sheffield*
> *Bus service 97 or 97A from High Street near T.J. Hughes (stop HS2)*
> *Services run every 10 minutes. Journey time: 20 minutes*
> *Ask for Beauchief Hotel*
> *Walk down Abbey Lane and turn at brown sign*

Sheffield: Bishops' House

With magnificent views south beyond Meers Brook (Boundary Stream) and over the city, the Bishops' House is the oldest timber-framed house in Sheffield. In 1500, when the Bishops' House was built, this was rural countryside where farming was the main occupation; a feature of the area was also the number of streams providing waterpower for the manufacture of scythes used to harvest wheat and hay.

The house is not grand enough to have been the home of two members of the Blythe family, who became bishops in the fifteenth and sixteenth centuries, as many people have believed, neither is it old enough for that. On the evidence we have it was another branch of the Blythe family who lived here: The initials and date 'WB 1627' carved on panelling in the hall refers to William Blythe, a farmer and a producer of scythes on a large scale. His wealth would certainly have been adequate to carry out the improvements made to the house in his generation.

Originally, Bishops' House was a traditional L-shaped Hall House; this consisted of an east wing with an open hall and kitchen and a west wing at right angles to it providing private rooms for the family. During building, the timber framing of these houses was pegged together on site and raised on to ground-level sills which were jointed into the corner posts of the frames. The frames were infilled with plaster spread on to oak strips set into the edges of the studs of the framing (a form of lath and plaster). It is the diagonal form of many of these studs which distinguishes northern Hall Houses from those in East Anglia where studs are traditionally vertical.

The open roofs of these early Hall Houses show the skill of the builders. Resting on the vertical posts of the building, and running across it, were massive tie beams; these have so-called King Posts jointed into their centre, which run up to support the ridge of the roof and take the weight of the roof covering.

The Bishops' House.

144

Over the years improvements were made: fireplaces were added, more glazed windows were inserted and there were early decorative features such as panelling and plasterwork.

The open roof tradition in the early halls began to disappear as ceilings were constructed; although people began to decorate the timbers used, it was the roof space created above and the warmth of the hall below that must have been the most welcome improvements from these changes.

The diagonal studs of the timber framing are conspicuous on the front of Bishops' House; also part of a local custom are the covings which support the overhanging gables and windows which can be said to be part of a 'Sheffield Style'.

The Bishops' House was restored and furnished for use as a museum in 1976. The house is normally open on Saturdays 10 a.m. to 4.30 p.m., and on Sundays 11 a.m. to 4.40 p.m. There is restricted opening in the winter. For further information call: 0114 2782600.

> For Sheffield Bishops' House take junction 33 off the M1 then the A630
> (Sheffield Parkway)
> At the roundabout turn left on to ring road A6102
> Continue past Gleadless Townend Supertram stop
> At Norton roundabout turn right onto Norton Avenue at the brown sign
> Follow brown signs for Graves Park, Bishops' House to the south-east corner
> of Meersbrook Park

> Or   Penistone Line to Sheffield
>   Bus service 20 from High Street near T.J. Hughes (stop HS2)
>   Ask for Norton Lees Road/Bishops' House
>   Service runs every 20 minutes. Journey time: 17 minutes

Sheffield: Botanical Gardens

Like so many of today's public institutions, the 19-acre Botanical Gardens originated from private initiative. In 1833 land on Clarkehouse Road was bought by Sheffield Botanical and Horticultural Society from the Wilson family, whose wealth came from their business, Sharrow Snuff Mills.

Gardens were laid out by Robert Marnock, who won a competition for a design; the opening took place in 1836 although only shareholders and subscribers enjoyed free access in those days. Today entry is free, the gardens being administered by Sheffield City Council.

Marnock's design was in the so-called 'Gardenesque' style, featuring winding paths, lawns, rock gardens and tree planted mounds. The three impressive Grade II listed curvilinear glass pavilions, with domed roofs and connected by lower colonnades, were designed by Benjamin Broomhead Taylor in 1836 and stretch for 90m. By 1939 the colonnades had been demolished and it became clear that a full restoration of the gardens, pavilions, offices, and curator's and caretaker's houses would have to be undertaken. The cost, including the pavilions with updated roofs and interiors was £6.69m, supported by the Heritage Lottery Fund. The restored pavilions were officially opened by the Prince of Wales in September 2003.

Sheffield Botanical Gardens.

The pavilions house a collection of plants from the temperate regions of the world: banana trees in fruit catch the eye near the entrance, with an enormous range of exhibits geographically located, many in flower, such as Agave (from which tequila is made). Others, such as Kashmir Cypress, are chosen for their outstanding foliage. At the end of the pavilion is a fine collection of cacti.

Following the restoration of the plant collection in the gardens, much of the original landscape design has been regained; the gardens are listed as being of special historic and architectural interest.

Plants are grouped into different garden areas, each with a different geographical or botanical theme. The national collection of Weigelas and Diervilla have their home here and the rose garden is especially beautiful.

Close to the main gate on Clarkehouse Road is a gift shop and nearby, in what was once the curator's house, is a restaurant and tea room.

Opening times:
Summer Weekdays:
Gardens from 8 a.m. Pavilions 11 a.m.
Summer Weekends:
Gardens from 10 a.m. Pavilions 11 a.m.
Winter Weekdays:
Gardens from 8 a.m. Pavilions 11 a.m.
Winter Weekends:
Gardens from 10 a.m. Pavilions 11 a.m.
For further information call: 0114 2686001.

For Sheffield Botanical Gardens take the A630 (Sheffield Parkway) off the M1 then follow the A57 towards Manchester
At Moore Street roundabout turn left onto Eccleshall Road
At the next roundabout turn right on Bronco Bank into Clarkehouse Road and main gate

Or   Penistone Line to Sheffield
Bus No. 30 from Church Street to main entrance
Service runs every 30 minutes. Journey time: 15 minutes

Sheffield: Cathedral of St Peter and St Paul

The ecclesiastical map of England divides the country into dioceses, each with its own cathedral; the name comes from the Latin 'cathedra', or 'a seat'. It signifies that it is the church of the diocese that has the bishop's throne.

Some of the 43 Anglican cathedrals, including Durham, date back to the Conquest, others, such as Chester, were added to the list after Henry VIII dissolved the monasteries and created the New Foundation. Liverpool, Guildford, Truro and Coventry (the latter rebuilt following its destruction in an air raid) are, of course all modern cathedrals; others were created in the nineteenth and twentieth centuries out of important parish churches. They were the result of a necessary division of some large dioceses where industry had developed and population had increased.

Wakefield, Bradford and Sheffield were among those former parish churches, Sheffield having being raised to cathedral status in 1913. As the parish church of Sheffield, it is in the heart of the city. Like the other cathedrals formed in this way, the church of St Peter and St Paul has been enlarged; it is not always easy to blend modern work with the old and controversy often follows.

At Sheffield the contrast of the traditional and the new is striking. For centuries the fifteenth-century crocketed spire had dominated the city skyline, so it must have been with some trepidation that plans were laid that would have given Sheffield a new church; with the outbreak of the Second World War the project was abandoned.

Sheffield Cathedral with its modern narthex.

The lantern, Sheffield Cathedral.

Eventually, the nave was extended westwards; this had already been rebuilt in the nineteenth century, so the church received a new west end. This may not appear obvious from the exterior, but what does catch the eye and the imagination is the narthex. This is an ancient type of entrance: a tall, projecting porch at the principal door with an enclosed vestibule. Built in the 1960s, its tower and its new stone can be seen with the original fifteenth-century tower and spire as its backdrop.

At the west end of the nave is the lantern, with glass in the roof by Amber Hiscott dated 1998; it represents the Crown of Thorns and its lively colours immediately catch the eye on entering the church. The nineteenth-century nave restoration was in the medieval style; beyond the chancel arch are the choir and sanctuary with a hammer beam roof dating from 1430. To the north and south of the High Altar are St Katherine's Chapel and the Lady Chapel.

The Earls of Shrewsbury were Lords of the Manor at Sheffield; the remains of their castle are below the Castle Market and neighbouring shops and streets. George Talbot, 4th Earl, built Manor Lodge as his principal residence. Now in ruins, this was one of the many places of confinement of Mary Queen of Scots (see p. 149).

The Shrewsbury Chapel on the south side of the Cathedral was built by the 4th Earl, who died in 1538; it is thought that although Worksop Manor was one of several properties he owned, he feared that the Priory there would be dissolved by King Henry VIII, so he chose Sheffield as his burial place. The tomb close to the High Altar is one of the most impressive in the country and has his alabaster effigy and those of his two wives by his side. He wears his armour, coronet and Garter mantle.

George Talbot, 6th Earl, is buried on the right in a handsome and elaborate tomb. It is said to have been built in his lifetime; the eulogy on its side is lengthy and fulsome no doubt to ensure that he would be remembered as he wished to be. He was the last of four husbands of the formidable Bess of Hardwick; she and the Earl were charged by Queen Elizabeth with the custody of Mary Queen of Scots and the stress placed upon them both is thought to have been one of the reasons for their estrangement and separation. He died a lonely, bitter man at Handsworth Manor near Sheffield; Bess lived on in the palatial new home she built, Hardwick Hall, and was buried in Derby Cathedral in 1608.

For Sheffield Cathedral take junction 33 off the M1 then A630 (Sheffield Parkway). Numerous parking areas on or near High Street/Church Street

Or   Penistone Line to Sheffield
From the Interchange Bus services 60 or 120
Services run every 10 minutes. Journey time: 5 minutes

Sheffield: Manor Lodge

In the sixteenth century, life at Sheffield Castle (see p. 148) was uncomfortable because of the cold, damp and dirt: that was Mary Queen of Scots' opinion when she was confined at Sheffield in the care of George Talbot, 6th Earl of Shrewsbury, and his wife Bess of Hardwick. But then, Mary was well known for her complaining.

The Talbots had such extensive properties in the Midlands and the North that they almost amounted to an empire; part of this was Sheffield and they had the manor house developed here from a medieval hunting lodge high up in the deer park – a more luxurious residence than the castle. Of the Manor Lodge little remains, save a wall of the Long Gallery and a few chimneystacks, as it was allowed to fall into disrepair by the next owner, the Duke of Norfolk.

The Turret House.

One of its famous visitors was Cardinal Wolsey on his last, fateful journey from Cawood (he never reached his goal of York) back to London. Another was Mary Queen of Scots, who was moved here from Sheffield Castle while it was 'cleansed' in the summer; although it was not really secure enough, it is thought that the Turret House was used to confine her. She was imprisoned at Sheffield for fourteen years altogether, having been allowed occasional visits to Chatsworth and Buxton; there was always a fear of conspiracies to help her to escape.

If the Turret House was just a gatehouse as has been suggested, it was a well-appointed one; it may have been a hunting tower where the Shrewsburys could go on summer days and the ladies could watch hunting activities in the park. The upper rooms are beautifully decorated and lend weight to that suggestion and that this was where Mary spent much of her confinement. The fireplace and ceiling have well preserved plaster mouldings showing the Talbot coat of arms. An exhibition is based in the Turret House that includes finds from an on-going excavation on the site, together with the history of the Manor House and its celebrated prisoner.

When Mary left Sheffield for good she was sent to Tutbury Castle in Staffordshire under a stricter gaoler, Sir Amyas Paulet; a number of plots were uncovered to arrange Mary's escape, the last involving an attempt to assassinate Queen Elizabeth. This discovery meant that Mary's days were numbered: she was tried and convicted of conspiracy against the Queen of England and executed at Fotheringhay in 1587.

Turret House plasterwork.

The Manor Lodge is open to the public. The Turret House is open by prior arrangement from Monday to Friday (9 a.m. to 5 p.m.). For more information ring: 0114 276 2828.

> *For Sheffield Manor take junction 33 off the MI then the A630*
> *(Sheffield Parkway)*
> *At the ring road roundabout turn left on to the A6102*
> *At Manor Top turn on to the A6135 (City Road)*
> *Pass the cemetery, then turn right on to Manor Lane*

> *Or   Penistone Line to Sheffield*
> *At the rail station take bus service 41 to Manor Lane*
> *Service runs every 8 minutes. Journey time: 10 minutes*

Pond Hill, Sheffield: the Old Queen's Head

This is a medieval gem, recorded as existing in 1582, sandwiched between the bus and coach interchange and Ponds International Sports Centre. What more contrasting neighbours could this pub have? The castle was once nearby and the pub, known in the past as Hall-in-the-Ponds, must have serviced the castle with drink. There were ponds here close to the River Sheaf; the Lord of the Manor made money through his monopoly of milling and these were probably mill ponds. They might also have been fishponds supplying the castle with food.

The age of the Old Queen's Head is confirmed by its timber framing and the covered overhang (jettying) of the first floor; there are practical as well as

The Old Queen's Head and a carved head in the bar.

architectural reasons for this, as the Shambles in York show. Decorative features like carved heads in the bar and close studs on the exterior walls suggest that the Old Queen's Head was important, its cost being borne by the Lord of the Manor.

It was originally larger than the two bays of today. A cross wing has disappeared and nineteenth-century road widening also reduced the size of the building. Restoration was carried out in 1993, but the Old Queen's Head remains the oldest pub in the city; it is exceptional in that it survives as an inn rather than an historic monument.

Did Mary Queen of Scots visit the Old Queen's Head when allowed out to exercise from her imprisonment? If she did, she might have been the 'tall mystery lady' seen there sometimes. We shall never know.

> *For Sheffield Old Queen's Head take junction 33 off the M1 then the A630 (Sheffield Parkway)*
> *At Park Square roundabout follow A61 signs*
> *Car park via left turn into Broad Street*
>
> *Or   Penistone Line to Sheffield*
> *Turn right out of the station and follow Sheaf Street*
> *At Pond Hill turn left, the pub is at the bottom of the street*
> *Access to Interchange on pub forecourt*

151

Sheffield: Arundel Gate, Millennium Galleries & Graves Art Gallery

The Galleries deserve every one of the many accolades they have received; completed in 2001, they have 1,800sq.m of exhibition space. Seen from Sheffield Hallam University across the road, the building is strikingly modern; the Café Azure at street level is fronted with glass and is so full of light that dining there is like dining alfresco. With a first class menu *and* table service, this is a place to be before or after a galleries visit.

On the upper floor (by escalator) is a shop and beyond is the astonishing Winter Garden, opened in 2002; also full of light from its curved glass roof, supported by huge arches, exotic plants, trees and bushes are encouraged to flourish. With its display of more than 2,500 trees and plants from around the world, it is the largest temperate glasshouse in any European city centre. There are information notices on plants for the real enthusiast.

Along this level is Sheffield's world-famous metalwork collection and the John Ruskin collection. Ruskin was not only a gifted artist, writer and a lover and critic of architecture, but a visionary who believed in the dignity of labour. He wanted to develop a society in which everyone would work, take pleasure in their labour and share their delight in its results.

Sheffield Millennium Galleries. Clockwise from above, left: Café Azure, Winter Garden, Metalwork Collection, Ruskin Collection. (Sheffield Galleries and Museums Service)

With the aim of achieving a just society, Ruskin founded St George's Guild at Sheffield in 1871; about 14 acres of land were acquired to form a working community to grow fruit. It failed, but he opened Ruskin Museum at Walkley in 1875 which housed a collection of paintings, sculptures, manuscripts, prints and other items which he felt worthy of inclusion. It was his influence that inspired William Morris and artists of the Arts & Crafts Movement, and it is entirely appropriate that the Ruskin collection should be at Sheffield's Millennium Galleries.

There are, of course, temporary exhibitions in craft and design as well as special programmes with loans from national museums and galleries. There are charges for these – otherwise entrance to the Millennium Galleries is free.

Graves Art Gallery

Originally intended to be part of a civic square development, a postwar change of plan has left the library and Graves Art Gallery in rather an inconspicuous location in Surrey Street, although adjacent to the Winter Garden at the Millennium Galleries.

Despite this, the Graves Art Gallery makes a memorable visit; the name of the gallery comes from Alderman J.G. Graves, a wealthy businessman who founded a mail order company and donated hundreds of his own works of art as a basis for the gallery's collection.

Three hundred years of European art are represented in the Graves Art Gallery, with a special emphasis on nineteenth- and twentieth-century painting. Fine examples of the work of Cézanne, Lautrec, Picasso and Spencer are exhibited here.

> *For Sheffield Millennium Galleries take junction 33 off the M1 then the A630 (Sheffield Parkway) to the city centre*
> *Follow brown signs for galleries and theatres*
> *Nearest car park is on Norfolk Street (reduced rate for gallery visitors)*

> *Or   Penistone Line to Sheffield*
> *Leave station, cross road and bear left*
> *Turn right on to Howard Street*
> *Galleries are opposite, at the top of the street*

Sheffield: Victoria Quays and the Sheffield–Tinsley Canal

The excitement that comes from a cruise on the Sheffield–Tinsley Canal today may not quite match the fevered anticipation on 22 February 1819 of the arrival of the first vessels at the Canal Basin, marking the opening of the canal. And today's tourist and leisure use of the canal is dramatically different from the purposes for which it was built.

Because of opposition from vested interests, there was a slow response to the obvious industrial advantages of having goods transported directly in and out of Sheffield by water in the nineteenth century. Even so, as elsewhere, businesses clamoured to set up along the canal and warehousing became an essential feature

Sheffield Victoria Quays: the Basin.

of the movement of materials. Had it not been for the canal, the city's steel and cutlery industries using cheap coal from the South Yorkshire coalfield might not have grown as they did. Apart from this, a new transport industry arose to build and operate the horse-drawn keels that loaded and unloaded at private wharves along the canal, or took cargoes to the warehouses at the Canal Basin.

It is sad to think that the prosperity of the canals lasted for little more than twenty years before the coming of the railways began to take over canal business. It seemed there was no future for the canals, but tourism has given them a new lease of life, not least for the Sheffield and Tinsley Canal.

The recent restoration of the Victoria Quays and the Basin attracted the boat people; a marina-type facility at both the Sheffield Basin and at Tinsley to provide an overnight service for water enthusiasts, improvements to the quays by British Waterways and the production of navigational guides has already brought success.

Heritage Cruises operate between Victoria Quays and Tinsley Locks between May and September. Commentaries explain what is seen en route and refreshments are available on board. A great deal has been done to refurbish the towpath and as there are several access points along the 5 miles to Tinsley, it is possible to walk the whole length in comfortable stages.

With notable exceptions, the state of the canals after the Second World War was woeful: neglected, abandoned even, many were no more than rubbish tips, leaking and becoming increasingly dangerous. When it was realised that, in spite of everything, they were an asset that should be preserved and developed as a public amenity, this all changed.

A cruise on the Sheffield and Tinsley Canal is a historic and environmental experience that shows its potential as a tourist attraction: on my trip, a wedding anniversary party added colour and helpings of cake were given to passengers. *Apollo* has been making the 1½ hour cruise from Victoria Quays for some years now; she was retired in 2006 and will be replaced.

The restoration of the Basin with its huge warehouses – Terminal (built in 1819), Grain and Straddle – was completed between 1993– 5; the arches facing the moorings also served as smaller warehouses for rail cargoes that passed through the Park Goods Yard above. Victoria station, now gone, was above here too.

Leaving the Canal Basin, cruises pass the recently built Basin Manager's office near to the swing bridge. On the left is the head office of Sheaf Works; this massive three-storey stone building with its handsome gable and rows of large windows is less like an industrial building than most. It would not disgrace a park in the Peak District. The Sheaf Works was the first to make use of the canal. After

Sheffield Victoria Quays: the Terminal Warehouse.

Sheffield–Tinsley Canal: the former Sheaf works.

Sheffield–Tinsley Canal: Bacon Lane bridge.

Sheffield–Tinsley Canal. Above: Damage to Bacon Lane bridge; above, right: crossing the aqueduct; right: Attercliffe cut and bridge.

passing under the railway viaduct, the Cadman Street bridge appears set at a curious angle; it has scars in its lower arches where tow ropes have gouged out the masonry.

The second and well-used railway bridge carrying the Midland line is followed by an industrial section of the canal, including Bedford Steels, a disused bone mill and an ironworks.

The Bacon Lane bridge is another curiosity, so difficult to negotiate that it became known as Needle's Eye and bears the marks of crowbars having been used to get keels through when the water was high.

Anyone interested in aqueducts will enjoy cruising across the Worksop road (the aqueduct was known locally as T'Acky Dock); beyond here industrial buildings give way to green banks, wildlife and fishermen – a different world.

Impossible to miss beyond the moorings area is the outline of the Don Valley Stadium and Sheffield Arena, built on the site of the Brown Bayley's Steelworks; beyond the Greenland Road bridge is the Tinsley Top Lock, one of seven leading to Tinsley and ending the cruise route.

The Meadowhall Centre is an enormous development here. For those walking, using the Supertram or the Penistone Line to reach this point, there is much more of the waterway to see by following the towpath as far as Halfpenny Bridge and the junction with the River Don.

Sheffield–Tinsley Canal: the Arena.

       For Sheffield Quays take junction 33 off the M1 then the A630 (Sheffield
       Parkway) to Park Square
       Turn right at the traffic lights, then next left to North Quay parking

Or   *Penistone Line to Sheffield*
       Turn right out of the station on to Sheaf Street
       At Ponds Forge walk up to Park Square upper level
       Cross the tram lines, go down to the lower level
       Look for the red brick Terminal warehouse and pass on its left to the Quays

Acknowledgements

I am deeply indebted to the many people whose kindness and enthusiasm for the Penistone Line project made its completion possible. Photographic and other credits do not properly express my appreciation for their generous research, information, advice and support which I acknowledge here with gratitude. Photographs are all the author's own, except where credits are given.

Our friendship continues and my apologies go to anyone not listed below. It is my sole responsibility for any errors or omissions in the book.

Brian Barnsley (ACoRP)
Holly Booker (RSPB)
Richard Casserley (Casserley Collection)
Alison Duce (Clifton Park Museum, Rotherham)
Judith Dyson (Denby Dale)
Christine and Robin Gallagher (Longley Old Hall)
Janet Goldsmith and fellow members of the Penistone Line Partnership
Kevin Grunill (Penistone Cinema Organ Trust)
Janet Hird (Bullhouse Chapel)
Graham Hurd (Kirklees Light Railway)
Barry C. Lane (Barry C. Lane Collection)
Gini Rodgers (Magna)
Richard Saward (National Coal Mining Museum)
Peter Sunderland (Haworth)
Alan Whitehouse (Holmfirth)
Claire Will (Sheffield Millennium Galleries)
Paula Worrillow (Priory Information and Resource Centre, Barnsley)

And finally thanks to my editor Simon Fletcher and his colleagues at Sutton Publishing, whose patience has been boundless.

Peter Thomas, 2007